DESTINY SEEKERS

DESTINY SEEKERS

Look Higher Than the Mountain

by
JAMES E. MOREL

DESTINY SEEKERS

Prepared and Packaged by
Illumify Media Global
www.IllumifyMedia.com
"Write. Market. Publish. SELL!"

Paperback ISBN: 978-1-949021-41-7
eBook ISBN: 978-1-949021-42-4

Printed in the United States of America

DEDICATION

First and foremost, I must thank my Savior and Lord who has been so faithful through the years in leading and directing my walk with Him and for the many dreams and visions with which He has blessed me. I want to thank my wife, Pamela for her love and patience; running the household and holding things together during my many hours in my office. I also want to thank my little band of faithful companions who met with me every Tuesday evening during the writing of this book. They took the time to discuss the book with me and do some editing. Thank you, Mike, Janet, Gary, and Stella for your support throughout this process.

CONTENTS

FOREWORD

As a congregation, we have always felt very strongly that the church should be the prophetic voice in the world. To be able to bring forth the prophetic, you must be able to hear the prophetic pronouncement of God. We have maintained the discipline of listening for His voice throughout our time together. In 2010, we began to hear what we believed to be the voice of the Lord directing us to change the way in which we walked before Him and worshiped Him. We studied the Scriptures with a renewed interest and found those ancient paths that I speak about throughout the pages of this book. We began the journey of returning to the Hebraic roots of our faith.

In my experience as a pastor, I have found that many Christians walk about with no more hope or vision for this life than those who are not Christians. I have a deep conviction that this should not be the case. Jesus said in John 10:10, "I have come that they may have life, and that they may have it more abundantly." The abundant life is His desire for all Christians. For the vast majority who do not enjoy this abundant life, there remains the question of how one acquires it. Jesus does not leave us to grope in darkness hoping to stumble upon the reality of His promises. He tells us exactly how to acquire this life and where it is found. Colossians 3:1–3, tells us plainly:

If then you were raised with Christ, seek those things which are above, where Christ is, sitting at the right hand of God. Set your mind on things above, not on things on the earth. For you died, and your life is hidden with Christ in God.

Our destiny is to be found in Him. He is the author and perfector of our faith (Heb.12:2). We are to live and move and have our being in Him (Acts 17:28). This abundant life became a reality for me and those that I have had the privilege of pastoring, over the past thirty years, when we were given the understanding that our Lord desires to communicate with His people, and He utilizes the gifts of the Holy Spirit within each of us to accomplish this. As it is written, "And He Himself gave some to be apostles, some prophets, some evangelists, and some pastors and teachers, for the equipping of the saints for the work of ministry, for the edifying of the body of Christ, till we all come to the unity of the faith and of the knowledge of the Son of God, to a perfect man, to the measure of the stature of the fullness of Christ [. . .]" (Eph. 4:11–13). We have found the prophetic gifting resident within people to be of tremendous value as well as the other gifts that the Holy Spirit imparts to individuals within the church. It was during the early 1980's when the gifts of the Spirit were being elevated that we began to understand it's importance. We found that being aware of those gifts was only the first step, asking for them and seeking the understanding of them was required. It was also very important to understand how to confirm whatever was coming forth in the prophetic realm. We learned that one cannot and must not be guided only by the prophetic, but also by the written Word and the revelation that comes through that Word. We accepted that the church was to be the prophetic voice in the earth and that as it is written, "Surely the Lord GOD does nothing, unless He reveals His secret to His servants the prophets" (Amos 3:7).

DREAMS FORMED IN CHRIST

Since man is prone to dream his dreams,
to look beyond the here and now,
to conjure with his mind,
the things that he would do and be,
then let my dreams be formed in You.
I say, then let this be,
for I, being me, cannot reach to heights
wherein you dwell,
I can only ask that I might span some distance
towards You with dreams made from this hope.
Ah, hope, that strange and elusive flow,
touching our inward man,
causing us to rise up to performance without measure.
The lack of which bringing men to their death,
before their bodies ever cease to function.
A strange thing—this charged up vessel,
filled with dreams and hopes to inspire more.
Have you known such a one?
They leap upon you with vigorous assaults of inspiration,
taking you by the hand into their dreams,
where with hope's light they dazzle you.
A strange thing this walking death is too,
Man, without hope, man without dreams.
Have you seen such a one?
Such longing in their eyes, such pain in their voices.

They too will take you by the hand and lead,
you away from that hope with which you dream your
dreams.
I am familiar with both, as are you.
The life abundant which hope supplies,
as radiant dreams.
The despair and death in dreams destroyed,
by hope's departure.
Is this not the perilous thing which man does fear,
more than all else?
That hope will not endure, till dreams are all fulfilled?
More than death itself this is feared, I think.
But, what can death rob me of,
if my hopes and dreams transcend the grave?
If I look beyond to life eternal in You.
There is no thief who can steal such hope.
But what of dreams that stay this side of the grave?
Surely hope's departure can bring them down,
And often will hasten the very hour of death itself.
That is why I say:
Since man is prone to dream his dreams,
Then let my dreams be formed in You.
For You are where no thief can dwell.
I hope in You, and from this hope my dreams are
formed.
I hear You speak, and thus my dreams are born.
I dream of a fullness of life in this Your world,
and of a place beyond to dwell where hope,
can be forgotten.
Where dreams are all fulfilled,
and in glorious splendor surpass the dreamer's visions.

For such a place, I hope and dream.

For such a time, I dream with hope.

Hope, we are told, is the anchor of the soul for every believer in Christ. Hebrews 6:19 states, "This *hope* we have as an anchor of the soul, both sure and steadfast, and which enters the *Presence* behind the veil [. . .]"

It is one thing for those in the world to lose their hope, a hope based in men, but another for Christians to lose their hope, a hope based upon the promises of God. These promises guarantee us peace with God (Romans 5:1), the assurance of a Helper and of a Comforter (John 14:16), as well as the promise of an abundant life which is our destiny.

The following chapters will be devoted to inspiring those Christians back to this abundant life that is based upon the promises of God and is secured by faith in those promises. It is the love for God that is shed abroad in our hearts by the Holy Spirit that will compel us to pursue these things. I state them here knowing that faith comes, and I believe can be rekindled, by hearing and hearing by the Word of God (Romans 10:17). Faith is a gift of God. Hope and faith, along with love, are the essentials of the Christian life. Without them we can do nothing pleasing to God, for to be without these things is to be without God in the world. God is love and our faith is in Him. "And now abide faith, hope, love, these three; but the greatest of these is love" (1 Cor. 13:13).

It is my prayer that His love abides in us and draws us away from the distractions of this world so that we may know our inheritance in Christ, and thus walk with assurance in the destiny that He has for us. We are to live in this world while not being of this world, which means not being devoted to this world. Let us begin with faith in this promise that comes to us from the mouth of the Savior and Lord Jesus Christ Himself, "Ask, and it will be given to you; seek, and you will find; knock, and it will be opened to you. For everyone who asks receives, and he who seeks finds, and to him who knocks it will be opened" (Matt. 7:7–8). In doing this we become *Destiny Seekers*.

PREFACE

"Thus says the LORD: "Stand in the ways and see, and ask for the old paths, where the good way is, and walk in it; then you will find rest for your souls" (Jer. 6:16).

Since the Lord began to speak to us about six years ago concerning these "old paths", ancient paths, our lives have changed dramatically. We have found the Word of God opened up to us in a new and living way. We have drawn closer together as a congregation. We have become a people who are truly understanding our destiny in a new light and how our destinies are tied together. Upon these ancient paths, we have known the love of God in a much deeper way. We have come to understand the plan of God for His people through the covenants and the Feasts of the Lord. We have learned how everything in the New Testament is derived from the Torah and the prophets and even the history of God's dealings with His people throughout time. This understanding has brought to us an appreciation for the Bible as a whole; the entire plan of God can be seen and understood. It has helped us to understand the world around us, the times in which we live, and what we believe is about to break forth in the earth as we await the second coming of our Messiah.

It is our prayer, as a congregation, that through the writing of this book you may be able to glimpse the reality we have known and are still experiencing. Our intercessory prayer team is praying for the church to once again be the prophetic voice in the earth.

The church that I now pastor is called New Covenant Christian Church of Laconia. It is primarily a teaching church, meaning that our emphasis is to equip the saints through teaching. While other churches may focus on missions or youth ministry, we are convinced that our focus is to be teaching the Word of God. Therefore, a good deal of time is given to teaching during our celebration of the Sabbath. Realizing that it may be difficult for someone new to the congregation to step into a series that is being taught or to hear words and phrases that are unique to the Hebraic understating of Scripture we have developed a glossary of terms booklet that we hand out to new comers so that they have ready access to words and terms used frequently. I am incorporating this information in this book so that those who desire to begin to study from this perspective may also have ready access to this information.

PART I
THE JOURNEY

CHAPTER ONE

SITTING AT THE WINDOW

The rain appears so gentle as it falls upon the ocean waves, forming thousands of dimples in the vast sea. The surf runs up upon the sand to catch all the drops it can and then hurries back to bring them into its depths. The sand is turning color, losing its pale white to a soft brown as the rain drops appear at first like freckles and then like a summer tan upon the long stretch of beach.

Growing up on the sea shore, I have spent much time at my window admiring such things as these. Just last week, as I was looking out the window, a sudden cloud burst hit the beach. I laughed to see all the people pull up their umbrellas and stuff their arms with blankets, baskets, babies, and folding chairs as they scurried up the beach to their cars or homes. I looked at the sand upon the beach, all marked up and ruffled from the activity and watched as the rain erased it all. In only a short time the sand was free of all evidence that anyone had tread upon it. The rain had settled the sands; the beach lost its memory and regained its beauty. I remember thinking how nice it would be if there were some kind of rain that could do the same for me.

This rain-washed beach served to give me hope that life, my life, could be so transformed by something that it would cleanse me as the rain did the beach. Though this hope remained with me through many seasons in my life, it had turned aside and I was left only with despair. You see the very thing that had given me this hope had too often turned against me. This gentle rain that brought the hope of a fresh new start too often became a raging storm that threatened and destroyed. How many times had I tried to keep the pleasures of the rain and disregard the despair of the storms, but I could no longer cling to the one and dismiss the other. My window had served to mirror the image of the storms in most of life's situations. Just as the gentle rain captured my heart and filled it with hope, it then betrayed me with the rage of its tempest to rob my heart of hope and fill it with despair. I learned that betrayal was too often the law that governed our lives. From my window, I saw this same cruel tragedy play out time and time again.

Once again, I looked from my window to the beach and saw young lovers embracing one another, so gentle, so satisfied, so hopeful about fulfilling one another's dreams. Then I saw how time and storm had taken its toll; for in another season, they would abandon gentleness and dreaming to become cruel and stagnant. I saw too from my window the newborn child laying between its mother and father on a blanket upon the beach. What joy the mother's face expressed; the child's father how he beamed with pride. Here I saw hope for joy and fulfillment. I imagined what it would be like to take your own child into your arms and hold him close to your chest like some treasure more precious than gold. However, once again, my smile was removed by the betrayal that soon must come. As I gazed down the beach a bit from this happy threesome to look upon the source of the noise that had distracted me, I viewed a mother shouting her disgust at her teenage daughter while her husband looked on with a familiar hopeless motion of hands in the air and his head shaking back and forth.

I've spent much time at my window observing some of the most important things in life. There is so much to hope for and yet hope is such a fleeting thing and so submissive to despair. More often than not, the gentle rain becomes the raging storm. The lovers consummate their love through marriage and then lose the very thing they had hoped to forever preserve. The blessing of the child fades into the past to become a source of worry, fear, and anger.

Another storm is raging out there on the sea and soon it will hit the coast crashing in on us like some wild beast thrashing about, full of anger and striking at anything in its path. I can see the ships being tossed about looking like bobbers at the end of a fishing line. They'll stay afloat; they always seem to weather the storms. They may get tossed about by the storm but it appears that they don't ever get hit like we do on the beach. We've just finished cleaning up from the last storm, but what's the use in complaining? There wouldn't be much to life if the storms didn't bring some calamity for us to scurry around. It seems like such a waste to sit here looking out the window waiting for the next storm. Not that anyone would confess to wanting the storms, but everyone seems to love telling their tales of woe after each one hits. At any rate, the storms will come. They always have and they will continue.

I have to laugh at the old man next door. He has a new remedy after each storm hits. Today he attached some so called "storm proof fixtures" to the edging on his roof. "No more problems with the roof", he says. The problem is, he can't seem to see that the biggest problem isn't with his roof. The foundation of his house is cracking because the wind and the rain are washing it away. He probably will still be muttering, "It will stand", when the walls come tumbling down. But his shingles will still be on the roof because he has "storm proof fixtures" attached to the edging. Ah, I guess he is typical of most of us here on the beach.

Look at all the time we spend fixing up after the storms and preparing for the next one. The whole world is geared up for storms. We buy insurance so that we'll have protection against loss due to a storm. We save money so that we can replace or add to our storm guards. What's the sense of it all? Where's the purpose? We spend years battling the elements, yet in one day a storm sweeps us out to sea. Oh yes, herein lies the purpose. We have a responsibility to the future storm watchers, our offspring, to ensure that they can follow in our footsteps as the victims of the endless process that gives definition to our existence.

Of course, we must be thankful for each calm before the storm. Like the rest period before round three in the ring, these are the sun-lit days full of carefree basking. What they really are though are days of self-indulgence and careless, rather than carefree, times of pleasure seeking. After all, we've earned a little fun in the sun, and there is no denying that there is some real fun to be had. One party after another offers a unique design to give you all you want out of life. These are called the times of your life and are supposed to make up for the tragedies that the storms bring our way. But remember, round three is coming up and the bell will sound again.

Sometimes, I wish that the storm destined to sweep me away would hit. It all seems so useless. We all do what we're supposed to do, what we have been taught and trained to do, but to what end? Maybe I'm different from everyone else, but it's depressing to me to maintain the status quo without knowing there's an end to it all, an end that is something other than being washed out to sea. Dreams are all vanquished with hope's departure.

The one thing that could make a difference is if there truly were a God. If you are real God, please show me. I've sat at this window from time to time during the past years with the same complaint only now I'm desperate to know, are you real? Isn't there anything more to life than this confused effort to battle against something over which we can't possibly claim a final victory? Please show me some reason for it all, give me some greater purpose for my life, or take it from me now.

CHAPTER TWO

THE FIRST STEP

The storm hit last night and raged through most of this morning. A lot of damage was reported down the coast a ways, and some loss of life. I read in the paper today that a few homes were completely washed away. I feel bad for the victims, but even worse for the ones who are left. They still have to go on in this endless tragedy brought about by the storms. Hopefully things will stay calm long enough for their grief to pass. I wonder what kind of comfort they'll be offered by their neighbors. They'll probably tell them that life must go on and even though it seems all is lost they can rebuild and carry on with their lives. Well maybe they will be comforted by that.

I see the old man's shingles stayed on the roof this time. It seems his storm proof fixtures worked after all. He's out there now raking up the broken branches and leaves that the storm brought down. I suppose I'll have to go out and do the same in my yard, but I'm going to wait until he's done so that I don't have to hear a sales pitch on storm proof fixtures for the roof.

Later that afternoon I did go out to rake up the yard and while I was cleaning up, I glanced up and noticed the most beautiful rainbow I had ever seen. The colors were unusually bright and the bow was much wider than I had ever seen. I looked around to see if anyone else was outside taking notice of the rainbow. It was beautifully stretched across the sky and seemed to frame a high mountain that was off in the distance. For some reason, it made me think of my conversation with God last night. As I thought of that conversation while gazing at the bow, I began to feel rather nervous or anxious inside. I sat down upon the sand, which was still a little damp from the storm, and propped myself up against the fence. I sat there looking at the bow and the mountain as if I were waiting for some meaning to float into my mind. After some time of pondering the sight before me, I was curious as to why the bow had remained for so long a time. Eventually my curiosity brought me to my feet and I began to walk towards the bow and the mountain.

Walking through a wooded area for some time, I found myself approaching the foot of the mountain. I stopped several times to peek through the top of the trees to see if the bow was still there. I would have ended my approach had it not remained, but each time I searched it out, it was still there, so I continued towards it. After several hours of climbing the slight incline through the woods, I reached a clearing just at the base of the mountain. The rainbow remained with a dazzling brightness across the sky. It was amazing to behold and it was nothing short of miraculous that it remained for such a long period of time. I knew that it must soon vanish since the sun was nearly ready to set. As it settled in the sky, it shone with a golden brilliance through the rainbow. Light and color spread across the whole sky appearing as if something was about to transcend out of it at the very top of the mountain.

I was now somewhat tired from my trek through the woods and a bit overwhelmed with the sight before me so I decided to rest in the clearing. I sat down upon the ground thinking to remain until the rainbow had vanished from the sky, then I would start back. I soon found myself laying there upon the ground with my eyes fixed upon the bow while falling asleep.

After some time, as if awakening from some strange dream that seemed to continue into reality, I found myself propped up against a magnificent old tree. It was a glorious old tree, unlike any I had ever seen. The boughs were covered with beautiful blossoms that scented the air as the breeze rustled the branches. Why had I not noticed this before? I determined that I had been so amazed by the bow that I just didn't notice the tree. It was set in a lightly forested area beside a flowing stream just at the edge of the clearing. I was somewhat bewildered that I hadn't noticed the tree or the stream earlier, yet, I was rather contented to be there and began to take it all in. There was a warmth that came from within me, making the soft cool breeze that was now blowing very soothing. I was aware of a most comforting presence that made it difficult for me to distinguish between reality and dream. I had never known reality to feel so safe. I had never known complete freedom from fear, but all my fear had now vanished and I felt hope returning to me. I felt compelled to look about me and to embrace with my eyes all that I could see. As I breathed in the sweet fragrance on the air, my mind was taking in a melody. "I love you, I love you, I love you", were the words attached to this mystical melody. These words and the melody were flowing into me, filling me, and pouring out of me. There was no resistance at all within me; I simply closed my eyes and loved for love's sake. I knew that I was being loved in a way that I had never been loved before and I responded to this love with my whole being. Never had I known such fulfillment or such purpose for my existence. I was a finely tuned instrument being played upon by a Chief-Musician. I was all poetry and melody. I became a love sonnet that had never been composed, but now I was being played with great intensity of emotion. There was no thought that could intrude upon me to disturb this chorus. It was as if I had been created only a moment ago and my mind was naked except for the pure and undefiled melody of love that flooded me.

It seemed that everything about me was so enchanted by the presence of this Chief-Musician that everything became a part of the song. A celebration was taking place, a grand and lively communion. It was as if the angels of heaven had descended to this place and were rejoicing over this new creation. The tree which I leaned upon was alive with excitement as its branches moved about yielding to the breeze, swaying to the melody. I too yielded to its swaying motion as I looked once again to the brilliance of the lighted sky. There was such fulfillment in surrender and yielding. The light inspired everything to be lifted upward. The grass stretched itself on tiny roots towards the light as the flowers curled their petals outward and upward. The gently flowing waters echoed the song in harmony with everything else as it waited to be lifted up in vapor toward the light. The whole sky was light and song and in brilliance it shone as far as I could see from north as far as north does go, and east and west and south the same. It seemed that heaven had invaded the earth. A heavenly orchestra played and I lost myself to it all as if I were part of a new creation that was unfolding. What happened in those moments entered my heart and will forever reside there.

I knew that I had met and was now in tune with this Chief-Musician. I knew that I had experienced God. Now I could allow hope to begin to form dreams within me. The future could be bright and full of purpose. He had heard my prayer and love was His answer. I could still but faintly hear a song sounding in my heart after all else had ceased. As I lifted my head upward, I saw this majestic mountain towering with great beauty against the sky. The sun was crowning the mountain as it began to set behind it. It was from this mountain that the stream beside me flowed down to meet the sea. As I looked upon the mountain I could see many settlements nestled in its side. Some of them were near to the stream and others were far from it. At that moment, my eyes were opened to see a vision. I knew that the vision was not reality and yet I knew that it was communicating reality to me. Set before me, in this vision was some of the history of the larger settlements upon the mountain. Also, I could see men of old who had been leaders in the various settlements, kneeling beside the stream and some were actually entering the stream. Some, not many, also left their place and ascended to the top of the mountain, but with resistance and great difficulty. Not only was I given to see these things, but somehow the knowledge of the conflict within some of the settlements and within some of the individuals was given to me as well. It was, as if in a moment, a lifetime was declared to me. In a moment, the history of the settlements upon the mountain was made known to me. But why? At first I thought that these men who ascended to the top of the mountain were to be my focus and I wanted to follow their ascent, but I could not, for my attention was quickly drawn away from them and to the settlements themselves, particularly to where they were located on the mountain. Some were higher than others, some closer to the stream than others, and some more fortified than others. I could see very large settlements as well as very small ones.

Then, suddenly, my attention was drawn towards the sea behind me. As I looked, I was astonished to see thousands upon thousands of ships upon the sea, great ships from long ago. Thousands upon thousands of men, women, and children gathered upon the beaches like colonies of birds clustered together. They did not look to the mountain, but only towards the sea, standing and waiting, as if for some new arrival to come and give direction. There were others leaving the beach and heading toward the path that led to the foot of the mountain. I wondered for a moment, would they arrive here? Would they hear the song? Would they see the things I had seen? Had they seen the rainbow as I had? Then suddenly the vision faded and the Chief-Musician began a melody, so I listened to hear what words would be put to the tune. As I listened I heard this song:

> Look higher than the mountain,
> Don't cast your eyes toward ground,
> Seek to pierce the clouds on high,
> With gaze towards heaven now be found.
> Don't stop at lofty peaks to dwell,
> Where man can climb and victory tell,
> But long to soar beyond man's means
> To places formed for God's redeemed.
> Look higher than the mountain,
> To where the flowing stream begins,
> The source is not in snowcapped peaks,
> It has it's start where all things end.

Was this to be my purpose, to ascend to the top of the mountain while looking beyond its peaks for a habitation? Was I to leave my residence upon the beach? I wondered what it all meant but decided to simply sing and let the composer disclose its secrets to me when He chose to do so. So, I sang the song to the melody that was given to me.

As the melody to the song continued, and as I sang the words given to me, my eyes were again opened to see another vision. Then, after a time, I grew silent waiting to understand if I were to return to my home on the beach until I had been given the meaning of the song. I began to inquire of this loving God who I had come to know only hours before. As I began to pray, my mind was once again opened to see into this second vision. This time I was taken in the vision to a place high above the top of the mountain to where the Chief-Musician dwelt. There I could see nothing except the One who had taken me to this place, the Chief-Musician Himself. Though I looked upon Him, I could not see Him clearly. As I dropped to my knees before Him, I saw Him dimly, as if viewing someone through dazed eyes just awakening from a deep sleep. I could not drop my eyes, but continued to gaze upon Him. He was clothed in light. As the light grew brighter and brighter I could no longer look upon His face, though I desired to do so. He appeared in a garment that looked to me like white linen spun through with gold. He wore around His waist, a golden belt. While I knelt before Him, I saw Him draw a sword from the belt around His waist. Holding my breath, I waited upon Him to see what He was about to do. He took the sword in His hand and placed it upon my right shoulder then over my head and upon my left shoulder. He never said a word to me, however, the song that had been given to me was being sung like some wonderful chorus that filled the whole place. Then the vison ended and I was made conscious of the fact that I had been placed by the stream. No understanding was given to me of the meaning of the vision. Although somehow, I now knew that I was to start my ascent up the mountain while remaining close to the stream, and so I began.

CHAPTER THREE

THE ASCENT

I followed the stream slowly advancing upward as it twisted along the mountain. My eyes searched for something that could be a point of reference for the end of my first day's journey. My mind returned to reflect upon all that had happened since I first saw the rainbow, and I wondered if I would ever again know the kind of experience that I had known in the clearing. My heart ached for it. I had hesitated in leaving the place where it had all occurred and hoped that I would return once again. I began my assent and as the first day's journey was ending, I laid down by the stream and slept.

As I woke the next morning, I heard the approach of someone just ahead of me. I looked to see who it might be and saw a man of about thirty years of age heading my way. He continued towards me until he stood just in front of me. He looked me in the eyes and said, "Brother, I've been sent to lead you for a distance up the mountain." I immediately felt at peace with this man who had come to greet me, but I wondered how he knew I was here and who had sent him to guide me. This was going to be a very interesting journey. He sat down upon a rock and asked me to do the same. Then he began to speak of his life prior to his ascent up the mountain. He had lived by the sea and was involved in many of the same things that I had also known while living on the beach. I was astonished that this man, whom I had never seen before, began to share his past life with me within five minutes of our meeting. It was by no means an innocent past; however, he went on to explain to me how God had forgiven him and set him free from the guilt of his past life and how he had been directed to the mountain just as I had. He explained to me an experience much like the one I had been through at the foot of the mountain. It was similar in many ways, yet also very different and unique to him. How wonderful, I thought, is this God who can bring such beauty out of such confusion and destruction in one's life? We sat there, two men who had been the victims of our own selfish desires, who not long ago lived, or rather existed, in fear of our true selves being discovered. Now we were like men newly created, given a purpose for our lives that would take us on a fantastic journey upon this mountain. We talked for some time, and then he invited me to begin my journey with him. This we did.

My desire for songs from the Chief-Musician was great and I would often request time to stop and sit by myself at the edge of the stream. I would listen for its melody and sing the song given to me back at the clearing. One evening while listening and singing the song, I began to understand it's meaning. I listened intently to each word and meditated on this new understanding that was flooding my mind.

"Look higher than the mountain."

I lifted my eyes as if in obedience to a command. I was to keep seeking the things above, never to settle only for that which the mountain could supply. There was much to learn on the mountain and much to be gathered while I ascended it. My goal was not to find a resting place upon the mountain, but rather to seek for the higher place, a place that I could not see with my natural eyes, but only know in the same way I had known it in the visions. I knew there would come a time when I would see clearly to abide in this habitation. Somehow, I also knew that this was my destiny. This mountain with all its splendor was the history of God and His people.

"Don't cast your eyes toward ground."

The ground represented man who was taken from the ground. I was not to look to the mountain or solely to man for the leading of my journey. My destiny was to be found in the Lord of the mountain. Certainly, He would use those upon the mountain to guide me. It was good in His sight that I should be upon the mountain. It was clear that my destiny was somehow tied to those upon the mountain. As if in disobedience to the command, I did cast my eyes toward the ground and looked downward at my feet upon the ground. These would carry me up the mountain but I had no idea which way to go. It was then that I began to understand that my trust in the Chief-Musician would take me to a path. This man that he had sent to guide me would lead me to this path. It was an ancient path that led up the mountain. It was the same path on which I had seen those men of old. The Chief-Musician was to be my true guide, but He would also give me those upon the mountain to assist me in my journey. He was the conductor and I was to listen for His songs. My eyes were to be stayed on Him.

"Seek to pierce the clouds on high."

These clouds that rested upon the peaks of the mountain prohibited me from seeing what it was that I longed to see: —His dwelling place, the place to which I had been brought in the second vision. These clouds appeared to be like some barrier that guarded the secret place of the Most High. How

I longed to pierce this barrier and to gain the knowledge of this secret place and to understand the mystery of it all. My mission, my calling, and my grandest goal in life was to make this pursuit above all else. I understood that if I sought this first and foremost, I would be given the knowledge and the understanding that I needed along the way.

"With gaze towards heaven now be found."

Heaven. This was His habitation. This abode was my true destination. I should always gaze towards heaven; always keeping it in sight, and mind, and allowing it to be my constant meditation, a peaceful place to dwell upon when things became difficult. This focus would give me the courage I needed when I would encounter various trials in my pursuit up the mountain. If I could keep in mind the blessed assurance of entering there, then everything I would encounter upon the path to its door could be viewed with hope. I had already been given a glimpse of what it would be like. I had been given just a taste in my glorious experience at the foot of the mountain, and this taste would keep me longing for more. Mine was an experience of the spiritual reality that existed for those upon the mountain.

"Don't stop at lofty peaks to dwell."

The understanding of this passage did not come so easily. I stood by the stream looking down into its waters. Then I looked up at the lofty peaks high upon the mountain. This is where the larger settlements were and as I looked at them, they seemed to be places of great achievements. I could see grand buildings shooting up from behind the walls of the cities. I began to reason that these settlements were so lofty in their appearance that they could easily capture those journeying with all their grandeur. Many, I supposed, had ended their journey there and had taken up residence within these towering fortresses.

I hoped that I would not. I knew that the path would lead me through them and that I was being warned not to stop my ascent, but to take from these places what I needed to continue my journey and move on. I hoped that I would not stop at these lofty peaks to dwell.

"Where man can climb and victory tell."

Certainly, a sense of victory rested in those who had climbed so high. A type of victory was told by the very existence of such lofty habitations high upon the mountain. I must admit that I was captured by the beauty of the structures nestled in the peaks with some of the larger towers rising into the clouds that topped the mountain.

"But long to soar beyond man's means."

How could I pass by such grandeur without being taken in by it? How could I ascend higher than the nobles who had built such tributes to God? I could not trust myself to step higher than they did, could I? The answer came swiftly as the words to the song rang in my ears, "Beyond man's means". I could not do it on my own. It was beyond my own ability. I was a man, just as those who had ascended the mountain before me. They had walked the ancient path just as I was. It was the Chief-Musician who would give me the means to pass by these monuments, or even to pass through them, without being taken captive by the stylish life offered there. If my longing was for Him, then He would sustain me and keep me on His path. Concerning "Man's means", I was to look for something higher than what man could achieve and boast of as his accomplishment.

"To places formed for God's redeemed."

Again, my thoughts were focused on the heavenly places and my mind was at peace. I knew that the Chief-Musician was able to lead me if my eyes stayed upon Him and His dwelling place. Though He inhabited the whole mountain through the songs of the stream and the message upon the wind, there was a place that He had formed for the redeemed much higher than the mountain. I was one of the redeemed. I had been redeemed from the mundane life on the beach. There I was hopeless, troubled with fear, and without purpose for my life. The mountain was for the redeemed also, but it was not to be their resting place; it was to be their means of ascending to the place that He had formed for an eternal dwelling. In this destined place, I would find the fullness of what I had experienced at the foot of the mountain. One more thought came to mind. At the foot of the mountain He had renewed the place of my dwelling. Would He renew the whole mountain and make this too a place for God's redeemed?

I stayed for a while by the stream and meditated upon all that I had taken in and the love exchange that had taken place at the foot of the mountain. Everything that I had just heard was for love's sake. I loved to sit and just think about the wonder of His love. It strengthened me to sing these love songs and it seemed as if my heart expanded to receive more of His love as I did so.

My brother was calling me and I arose to meet him as he walked towards me. He told me that he had gone to speak to other brothers and sisters who were his companions on his journey up the mountain. I asked him if he had been called to go higher than the mountain as I had been. He told me, yes. I then asked him why he was not ascending and why he was residing in one of the settlements. He said that the journey on the ancient path was the journey of a lifetime and that we must settle on the mountain from time to time and learn the things that were necessary for further ascent. I did not understand what he was saying. It sounded as if it was contrary to what the Chief-Musician had called me to do. Knowing that he had been sent to guide me up the mountain, I asked him to explain his meaning. He said that the Chief-Musician would continue to give us songs and visions and that He would never stop calling us up higher; however, our journey would take a lifetime and during our ascent we needed all the things necessary to live on the mountain. He said that I would understand more once he had brought me to his companions. They would teach me certain necessary things to know in order to climb the mountain in safety. We walked a very short distance to where they were gathered. As we approached, I heard a most beautiful chorus being sung by this group of people. We entered in among them and joined in the song. I had never heard the song before so I could not join in with the words but I joined in the celebration by weeping at the beauty of it all. The same presence that had surrounded me at the foot of the mountain was now surrounding me and filling me here. A love song was being sung by all who were present. I knew they could hear the Chief-Musician playing a melody in their hearts and their voices resounded in response.

My guide and I went on for some time before we ceased and sat down together. There were others who were new to the gathering that day and we took some time for introductions. Then a man stood up, drawing our attention and quieting the assembly and began to speak. As if for my benefit alone, he laid out a plan for climbing the mountain. He shared his own experiences in his pursuit of the top, cautioning us about making permanent camps in places that seemed to offer comfort and security. He had lived in such a camp for some time and told us of the danger of settling down rather than continuing on. He also spoke of the danger of climbing alone with no one for support in the rough places. He pointed out the importance of the song that each individual was given by the Chief-Musician and that His true delight was a harmony of those songs as we all shared them one with another. He continued in exhorting us to learn from the experienced climbers, those who were always in pursuit of the high places. When the time grew near to break up, we were ready to begin a new day's journey up the mountain. I did not fully understand all that had taken place that day or all that was said for our benefit and instruction, but I was very pleased that I would ascend the mountain with so many who loved the Chief-Musician as I did.

I felt safe with my new-found brothers and sisters. As we began to climb, I understood from some of the others that this was to be our pattern. We would come together often to celebrate and share our songs and we would go from there to pursue our goal. I soon found that my times alone sitting by the stream would be very important to me as well. It was here that I was most in tune with the Chief-Musician and here that I was most often lifted to heights beyond the clouds, both in visions and in dreams. What we would celebrate in our corporate anthems was the fact that each one of us was so loved and so cared for by the Chief-Musician. It was our individual communion with Him that gave each of us real purpose.

I soon realized that the physical pursuit we would embark on together would be a difficult one. If I did not sit by the stream often, listen to the melody, and sing the songs given to me, I would lack vision for the climb. I could not ride long on the vision of others. I was most strengthened and nourished by my personal interaction with Him. The instruction in the gatherings would take on clear meaning during the times by the stream. The mountain was filled with truly wise and noble men, many who had traveled to the lofty peaks and back, but I was to look to the Chief-Musician for the melody and the words, not to these men only. Often, they could help me understand the song when I was weak or fearful or confused, but they were not to be the source for me; only He could lead me on. Taking all that the mountain was meant to offer to those ascending was good and wise to do if it did not halt our ascension. However, it would never be enough if I were to pierce the clouds on high. So, with this revelation I lifted my eyes and looked "higher than the mountain" as I rested by the stream.

CHAPTER FOUR

THE LARGEST CAMP

The sun had just set over the mountain while the cool air sweeping past me was soothing as it left the woodland and headed down to the valley below. I lifted my head to face into the breeze and closed my eyes. My soul rested as I allowed the breeze to carry my thoughts away. Then, at peace within myself and content with my position on the mountain, I laid down to rest.

As I slept, a dream was given to me. In the dream, I found myself in one of the largest camps on the mountain. I stood a short distance from the front of one of the camp's large structures and I could see many people very casually entering it. This went on for some time while I stood and watched. Suddenly, as if struck by lightning, the structure exploded into flames. I was terrified for the people who had entered the structure. Why weren't they running out to save themselves? Were they all trapped inside? Helplessly watching the building burn, I stood and desperately looked for someone to come and give aid to those inside the burning building. Turning and looking to my left, I beheld a man calmly approaching me, seemingly unaware of what was taking place. I began to cry out to him, trying to draw his attention to the building and the fact that there were people inside. He looked at me, reached out his hand, and placed it on my shoulder. I quieted almost immediately at His touch as I looked into His face. His eyes spoke to my heart and I knew His voice. He was the Chief-Musician. I was now so captured by His penetrating gaze that my thoughts of the burning building had almost completely left me. Releasing me from the intensity of His presence, He pointed toward the building, directing me to enter. The flames, as if by some miracle, had all died out leaving the outside of the building all charred and black. And inside? I did not know what I would find inside. I knew that I must enter this tomb to see if anyone might have survived such an awful tragedy.

As I approached the steps, my mind conceived all manner of hideous sights waiting for me inside. Just before entering, I turned and looked back at the Chief-Musician hoping I might be released from this terrifying obligation. He smiled and encouraged me with a gesture of His hand to enter. With much fear, I ascended the steps, one at a time, trying to sustain my composure or somehow gain some courage with each step. The doors were opened, one hanging upon a single hinge, the other simply standing, ready to fall at the slightest touch. My heart pounded and raced within me until I thought it would burst. As I gasped for breath, I could not draw it deep enough to satisfy me. Once inside the entrance way, I heard what sounded like muffled humming. I thought, someone is alive, they're groaning in pain, what will I do? With light hope and overwhelming terror, I quickly stepped forward and grabbed the handles to the inner doors and flung them open. Then, as if paralyzed, I stood holding open the doors. I could not react to what my eyes beheld except to stand gazing at the sight. There before me were the people who had entered the building, laying prostrate on the floor, quietly singing and weeping. The inside of the building was dazzling, as if of pure gold. The place was full of light and no darkness could be seen in it. As I stood in amazement at this sight before me, I turned to draw some explanation from the Chief-Musician. He was no longer there. My dream ended. The only thing I knew with any certainty, concerning the dream, was it was the Chief-Musician who had authored it, and it was given as a direction for me. I would one day enter this camp of which I had dreamed and enter this same structure within the camp. But I wondered; how would it all be possible? How would I get there? What would I do there? What was the purpose for it all? Again, as with the first song, and the vision that had been given to me, I would wait for the author to make its meaning clear.

I continued on with these brothers and sisters who had received me as a companion for some time. We would often gather in general meetings as well as smaller, more personal and intimate groups, both for the purpose of celebration and instruction. The days with these brothers and sisters were wonderful times that I enjoyed immensely. They were second only to the times by the stream where I would spend hours conversing with the Chief-Musician about the meanings of the songs, the visions and the dreams, as well as seeking an understanding of the things shared in the meetings. It was at the stream where I learned what was most precious to me, who He really was, and why He loved me and choose me to make this climb.

One time when I was sitting by the stream and considering such things, I looked down the mountain. I didn't often look back because I was always so captured by the majesty of the peaks higher up and still so enchanted by the melody of the stream. However, this time I gazed back and again saw the sea, crowded with ships. There was a tremendous storm upon the sea that appeared to be battling the tiny ships. The ships looked to be fighting for their very existence as they were tossed and turned, and driven and battered to the point of almost colliding with each other. There were also the people on the shore still standing looking to the ships to bring them some good news or some new arrival, or waiting for their ship to come in. I was saddened by what I was seeing. Compassion rose within me for this countless herd that was before me. I realized then what privilege had been given to me. I had lived as they, without ever turning to look upon the mountain, dazzled by the endless sea and all my hopes cast upon its waters. But as for me, I was turned around to see a far greater sight. At the thought of this, I marveled. I wondered why I had been chosen to know such love. Tears began to run down my cheeks and my heart began to burst into a song of thanksgiving. I loved to sing of the Chief-Musician, because I knew that He delighted in my songs. I loved the songs that He would birth within me because they would express the feelings that I had deep inside me. I loved the dreams He formed and the visions He presented to me, as they brought such purpose into my life. I loved the mountain and the new family He had given me. Most importantly, He had given me a love for myself, and for the life I now lived upon the mountain. Here I sat, looking out upon the sea and weeping over the new love I had been given, and singing this song of thanksgiving.

Walking down the road of my past gone by,
Looking for a reason and wondering why,
Why have You loved me the way that You do,
Why have You taken the time?

Your love goes on and on and on and on and on,
Filling me with hope and joy and song.
Your love goes on and on and on, and on and on
And it's Your love that's making me strong.
Remembering the day that I first met You,
Felt so good inside finding You to be true,
It's then that Your Spirit started making me anew,
I love You because You love me like You do.
Your love goes on and on and on and on
Yes, it's Your love that's making me strong.

I would spend time with the others and the times of meditating by the stream. I devoted hour upon hour reading and studying a book that had been given to me about the history of the mountain and those who had traveled on it. I learned that they had addressed the Chief-Musician as Lord and so I would begin to as well. What was of special interest to me was the part of the book about a time when the Lord descended to the mountain and walked the same path that I was now walking: The Ancient Path. This comforted me because I knew He was familiar with all the best ways of making it to the top and then beyond. I read of how He too loved the stream as I did, and I was encouraged to read about the many times He spent by the stream. He also became my example for always looking higher than the mountain. Though He spent much time expressing His love for the mountain, it was clear that His eyes were always fixed on things above. He came intentionally to lead all the inhabitants of the mountain, and even those on the beaches and upon the sea, to those heavenly places. All who would follow Him, He welcomed. How is it that so few would understand His words?

It saddened me to look upon the mountain and see how many stopped and made permanent camps there, rather than going on after the Lord. They had become so content with the things of the mountain that they no longer sought to go higher. Many of them, it seemed, began to live just as they did on the shore, taking up old habits and living as if they had never heard the songs upon the mountain. Their camps were filled with songs about the land beyond, yet they could not see the need to let go of and leave what they had built for the sake of climbing on. So, they became blind to the heavenly vision, easily casting it into a mold that pertained to a people of another time. They forgot about the ancient path and built a kingdom of their own. This frightened me because I knew that I must enter one of the camps where such was the case. Would I too become blinded?

Now, much time had passed since the dream about the burning structure. I had even forgotten there was a dream. One evening I was invited to attend a meeting that was to include a large group of people from the different camps. Not only was I surprised that such meetings occurred, but I didn't really want to attend. I had heard that there was so much bickering between the camps, that I just wasn't sure what to expect. Well, the meeting was a celebration similar to what I had become used to. It was both surprising and comforting to me that it was. After the celebration, another meeting with just the occupants of one camp was planned. For some reason, I was invited to attend, so with great apprehension I accepted. This was one of the most ancient and largest camps upon the mountain. Its structures rose high into the air and stood like Father Time, staring down, daring a challenge by any who were indifferent to its stroking of the clock.

When I and those who accompanied me arrived at the camp, we entered one of the structures within. I simply flowed along with the crowd, trying to be as inconspicuous as possible. Nervousness choked my breathing as I waited for time to dictate my departure. As the meeting went on, I began to call upon the Lord, quietly, within myself. To my surprise, He answered in a voice that only I could hear, with the swiftness of a Symphony Conductor, cueing in my instrument. "The dream" He said, "This is the beginning of its fulfillment". Without any further instruction needed, my heart sunk as I understood immediately what I was to do. An attendant of the camp was present and I was to share my dream with him. One after another, thoughts of resistance to the Conductor's cue entered my mind.

The attendant will reject me completely, I thought. He will think me crazy. He will rebuke me and humiliate me before all these people. Oh, if only I could escape this; if only there were another way.

However, it was clear what the Lord, the Chief-Musician, the Conductor, had chosen for me. The direction was inescapable and I was compelled to follow my cue. How else could I return to the stream and listen to its song if I were unwilling to play my part in the symphony? So, I approached the attendant and shared my dream with him. He must have seen the shock upon my face when he replied to my words with an expression of acceptance and gratitude.

He lifted his arms and said, "Wonderful, you're just the man I've been waiting for. I've been asking the Lord for just such a thing as you have described through your dream."

I wondered how he could possibly understand the dream that I had not understood at all. He then invited me to join

47

him by the stream in two days so that we might together wait on the Lord for further instruction. After the meeting, I left and immediately went by myself to the stream. There I spent the night.

As the weeks rolled by, the attendant and I spent a great deal of time by the stream. I was beginning to gain an understanding of the dream as its figurative language unfolded into actual experience before my eyes. The Lord was gathering together, one after another, those who would be co-laborers in the task we had agreed to undertake. Unknown to us, the task that we agreed upon was to be much different than the one the Lord intended. I became more and more aware that we were like agents in some top-secret plan that only the Lord really understood. We played our parts as far as we knew, or thought we knew, yet we were unaware that our actions would cause results unintended by any of us.

I felt that I had to put off climbing the mountain for a time to accomplish a work that would please the Lord. This meant that I was to leave my brothers and sisters with whom I had traveled thus far, while they were to continue on. It was a very sad departure; one that I made with much heartache. As I said, the hidden meaning of the dream was unfolding before me, little by little. The structure that I saw in flames I now knew was the very structure that I would live in while staying within the large camp. The outward appearance of the structure, which represented all the tradition and formalism of this camp, would be destroyed by the flames which was the very essence of the Lord, Himself. As the tradition and formalism were burned up, a transformation would take place not within the structure, but within the people who were to be the true dwelling place of the Lord. He would dwell within them as they yielded to His melody. It was the people that would emerge changed. I was to stay for a time with those people and within that structure while the flames accomplished their purpose. One thing I knew was that the flames without, would create a heat within. Not too long after we had begun to walk this out together, it grew very hot. I was very unsure of my overall purpose in all of these happenings; however, I knew with certainty that I was to remain. One of the things that disturbed me the most was the distance of this camp from the stream, and that so few of its occupants had ever traveled to the stream. Many of them, I discovered, had never been to the stream because they did not know it existed. The "forefathers" were not faithful to tell them of the stream. There was always so much going on inside of the camp that they, like the people on the beach, existed unaware of the lack of real purpose in their lives: a purpose that would be birthed within them by the Lord. The only difference between them and the people on the beach was that these people worked together on the maintenance of the structures within the camp in addition to attending to their personal tasks. Yes, they had a purpose, but it was not at all fulfilling. Consequently, they had many of the same grievances as those on the beach and the sea. The camp attendant, the one who visited the stream with me, knew of the stream because some time ago he had visited it with some others. He was excited about the stream and desired for others within the structure, where he served, to know of its existence. He had experienced the song from the Chief-Musician as it sounded from the waters to him. I found one thing to be different with him. He was trying to fit the words of the new song to an old melody. It sounded awkward when he would sing it. The new words just didn't fit the old tune. Others within the camp did not recognize this because it became more and more like the old songs they had been singing within the camp. It was not fresh and new and full of life giving melody. More and more of my songs and the songs of the attendant were not compatible and this did begin to become evident to the people of the camp after a time. It was made clear to me by the Lord that I was not to criticize the attendant, but I was simply to sing my songs. As they heard me sing and desired to know where my songs came from, I was to show the people the way to the stream. These same people within this camp were very loyal to the attendants. Every word of direction I uttered would be checked out with the attendants. This was very frustrating to me because I felt that I often knew the way better than they, but only because of the Lord's leading. I was beginning to spend much of my time at the stream complaining to the Lord rather than singing songs to Him. I would go to the stream less often now than I used to, and I was aware that I was becoming engrossed in the traditions and formalisms of the camp. More and more of my time was spent on tasks that had little to do with the Lord. In my attempts to be obedient and not criticize the others, I began to submit to their traditions and, as a result, was compromising my time with the Lord. What I had feared had come to pass. I was beginning to settle in. I thought little about the Ancient Path and ascending the mountain. I wondered often about my brothers and sisters who moved on while I stayed here. I still cherished the memory of past times with them, and, I would speak much about those times with these new people. I began to wonder if I had compromised too much by not criticizing the attendant. Even the times at the stream seemed to offer no council and no new songs. There were frequent times of celebration just like I used to enjoy with my travel companions, yet these celebrations were not surrounded with the embrace of the Lord in the way I had experienced with the others. We just didn't flow together in a song of gladness to the Chief-Musician. There was always a formalism and structure that seemed to hinder our celebration from becoming jubilant. It was as if we were sitting beside the stream, but the stream was polluted with the traditions of the camp so that we could not see its clearness. Its flow was somehow obstructed so that we could not hear its melody distinctly. No one would bring to the celebration the freshness of an individual love song to sing in harmony with each other, making our celebrations so wonderful.

I feared what would become of me should I remain here much longer. I began to resent being led into this place. Though I was growing in my love for the people around me, I was growing in bitterness for remaining in the camp. I felt trapped, and longed for someone to lead me away. To whom could I turn? In my bitterness, I did not travel to the stream but stayed within the structure and called out to the Lord from there. I learned of the emptiness of those who dwelt within the camp. They lived on old water that had long ago been drawn from the stream. It only served as a reminder of days past when the stream gave life and songs to others. I became desperate for those waters again and I cried out to the Lord to release me from this camp so that I might again ascend the mountain. To remain here would be death for me; the same kind of living death I had known existed on the beach. Not knowing what else to do, I did continue there for some time, still feeling trapped. I grew in favor with the people, for time gave me opportunity to share with them my songs, the ones I had once sung. It seemed, so long ago.

I had been told by the Lord not to criticize, but only to speak what I knew to be truth both about the stream and the call to look higher than the mountain. That is what I did and the people began to listen to me. Some of them even began to grow angry because they felt that they had been made to live on polluted waters. I tried to quell this anger and to focus their attention on the purposes for our lives in the will of the Lord. They became my friends, and together we began to long for the fresh waters of the stream and to hear its songs. Now they would often ask me to sing for them and to repeat the songs that I had heard. As I lived with them and sang, I began to learn some things that I might never have learned had I not been sent there. Recognizing this, I determined to trust the Lord again, for I hadn't realized I had stopped trusting Him. I saw, perhaps for the first time, that the reason I had stopped visiting the stream was because I did not trust the Lord to guide and direct me. When things went well I would sit by the stream and sing for hours. However, when things looked bad I would stay within the camp and not visit the stream as a way of punishing the Lord, or so I thought. Now I had to consider that my being sent there had a twofold purpose. Not only were the people of this camp to be changed by the fire, but I too was to be changed by these flames. It was here that my doubts and fears were exposed.

The things that I had thought were shed at the foot of the mountain were still within me. My heart was burning within me as I was forced to face my failure. How could I despair after the wonderful things He had brought into my life? Yet, I did despair. Now I reasoned that I must face the fears and doubts, somehow overcome them, and return to the stream and the Lord. The presence of fear and doubt became more obvious the longer I neglected the stream. They became like wolves howling in the night, a distant eerie sound that breaks the peaceful silence of the night's rest. My eyes were opened to see His purpose in leading me here. I felt the coldness of the empty structures, the loneliness of the masses who gathered in shallow friendships, still holding on to their fears and doubts, longing for someone to touch their heart with understanding instead of judgement. I would not have believed that this could happen on the mountain unless I had experienced it for myself. I had to overcome the fears and doubts. However, I knew that I could not overcome them on my own. I had to first return to the stream and the Lord so that He could overcome them in me. I had been singing my songs and become indifferent to the message contained within the songs. Was I back at my window looking out over the sea again? Had I not gained anything? Had I failed? Had I been downcast looking at my feet, trusting in myself rather than looking to Him? I stood to my feet weeping, running, and calling on the Lord. I ran as fast as could to the stream and threw myself down upon the ground at its edge.

"Please forgive me," I cried. "I've tried to do what you wanted but I've failed and I'm afraid and confused. Please forgive me, please restore me."

With tears streaming down my face, I lifted my head toward the heavens. As I did, I beheld the Lord walking toward me, walking on the waters of the stream. He was dressed as I had seen Him before. With His arms outstretched, He came and took me to His chest. He held me and said, "Know that I love you." I could not control my sobbing. When I realized that He was weeping with me, my heart melted within me. At His embrace, all had left me but love, no fear, no doubt, only love.

It seemed like hours had passed in His arms. At His departure, I laid beside the stream exhausted yet content.

As I slept, another dream was given to me. In the dream, I accompanied the attendant of the camp, with whom I had been laboring, to the back of the altar that was erected within the structure where we would hold our celebrations. While behind the altar, the attendant reached up and took hold of a shepherd's staff. He then looked intently into my eyes with no expression upon his face that I could read. He passed me the shepherd's staff and turned from me and walked away. I was left there holding the staff when my dream ended. I was not to understand the meaning of this dream until I had walked it out in actual events taking place months later.

Though my communion with the Lord was somewhat clouded by the rituals and routine of daily life within the camp, I knew that I had more purpose in life than those with whom I dwelt. Once again, I had learned how vastly important it was that we look higher than the mountain. My purpose was in ascending the mountain even though there were to be delays in the process. Having now entered this camp, I could see one thing more clearly. All the camps upon the mountain had in times past drawn from the waters of the stream and had listened to its songs and collectively had a great deal of knowledge concerning what the stream could offer. However, we as individuals were limited to dwell in one camp at a time and could not benefit from the knowledge contained in all of the camps because they were different, separate, and independent. I also saw that much of what remained of the melodies and the songs in each camp had become celebrations of times past rather than joyful songs of looking to the future. The people who drew only from what was within the camps, were only as alive as the camp in which they dwelt, unless they frequented the stream. The further the camp was from the stream, the more difficult it was for them to visit. Those who often visited the stream went in and out of certain camps, but were few in number and often looked upon with indifference. Some people did not settle long enough to form permanent residence in any camp. These were the high climbers who, like nomads, traveled with few possessions, were intent upon moving toward the final resting place and would not settle for less than the dwelling place of the Lord Himself. Such climbers were the ones with great vision, who did indeed look higher than the mountain. I knew I would become a high climber as long as I sat often by the stream and listened to the songs of the Chief-Musician calling me on. Here, at the stream, my desire would be rekindled over and over again, and stay alive.

As I continued on in the camp, two events emerged together to bring about the unfolding of the meaning to the last dream. However, as these events took place, they did not allude to the dream until the final moments of the last event's completion. The first event was a series of complaints on the part of the people against the attendants of the camp. Because of what I had shared with them about the stream and the Chief-Musician, they desired to begin to climb the mountain and to leave the camp. They called upon me to be their guide. This was very unsettling for the attendants and for me as well. Though I wanted to continue on myself, I was terrified that anyone should follow my leading. I did not want the responsibility of these people wanting to leave the camp. I had heard that the Lord had led others into various camps, such as this one, to bring the songs of the stream. I thought all along that such would be my task. I would bring to a camp some freshness from the stream and then depart to rejoin those with whom I had first walked. My leading some of the occupants out of the camp was another thing altogether.

The second event occurring during that same time, was that the attendant, with whom I had been laboring, was being transferred to another structure upon the mountain. You see, he had simply exhorted the people to look to me for guidance. Before he left, he had publicly given the care of the people over to me and two others within the camp. Both he and I were unaware that this meant the shepherd's staff had been passed. It had taken place at that time. However, the Lord was aware of what was actually taking place, for He had conducted the whole thing from beginning to end.

Soon after the attendant left, I decided things were getting too uncomfortable. The fire from the first dream, was certainly raging outside at this point. I headed with haste towards the band of brothers and sisters with whom I had first traveled, thinking my task had been accomplished within that camp. Much to my surprise, I discovered that many of the people within the camp to whom I had been closest, followed me out. So, I departed the large settlement, not alone as I had entered it, but with a company of followers as well as a shepherd's staff in my hand. Thus, both dreams were fulfilled. The fire of the Lord's love had engulfed a people, burned away their tradition and their rituals, and made of them a people with a vision for the high places. As for me? He made me a shepherd and a guide to the heights beyond the mountain peaks.

CHAPTER FIVE

LOST IN THE FOREST

I tried to relinquish the role as guide from the very first. I felt tired and worn from the days within the camp. I wanted to just lie by the stream and drink in the songs and the melodies of the waters. Although I told the Lord that I wanted to serve Him, I did not want the concern for these people to become my burden. I soon found that things would never be the same. Wanting desperately to rejoin the others who had gone on ahead, I decided to take the group with me and enter in among my former companions once again. We would all walk together was my thinking. As I tried to lead these people into the midst of those with whom I had first traveled, I was refused entry in among them. I shared all that had taken place within the large camp and I was told by the guides that the Lord had guided me into the large settlement to become their guide out. It was evident they said, by what had taken place. I was counseled to remain on the ancient path with the people who had come out of the large camp with me, staying close to the stream. However, the two groups would not be combined. This was the design of the Lord they insisted. I wondered why was this happening to me. It now had become more difficult for me to ascend, not at all like when I had first begun.

My vision was beginning to fade due to the disappointment of being turned away. Again, I found myself unsettled by the song that once was so soothing to me. I told the people to set up camp and that I would return in a few days. In a frenzy, I rushed to the stream where I spent many days by myself until I could come to grips with the reality to which I had to surrender. For the first few days by the stream, I could not hear the Musician's melody because I was so engrossed in my own song of woe. Then, as I remained by the stream, my anxiety began to wane along with my great concerns. Once again, I could hear the Lord, and His song began to calm me like a lullaby. Curling up by the edge of the stream, I rested my mind and remembered my last thoughts before falling asleep: "Lord how can you use this weak vessel?"

The approach of one of the brothers woke me out of my slumber. It was my first guide that the Lord had sent, in what now seemed a lifetime ago. He came back to check on me, to see how I was doing. He came to speak with me about the task that was before me to guide this people up the mountain. With compassion, he encouraged me and spoke of a time in his journey up the mountain when he had faced similar difficulties. He spoke of the Lord and of how He had been faithful to minister songs giving him hope, courage, and direction during his struggle. He encouraged me to sit often by the stream and listen for the songs. He offered to be a help to me as often as I needed it. He invited me to meet him by the stream or to enter in with his companions for counsel from time to time. He would continue to travel with those of whom I began my journey, as well as to serve as one of their guides. He asked that he might pray for me before we parted. I said yes and he laid his hands upon my head and began to prophecy these words from the Lord, "As you are faithful to seek me, I will bring to you understanding and strength for your way upon the mountain." His words lifted me, and as he walked away I asked the Lord to forgive me for ever doubting that He would supply all that I needed. I could see now that He would be faithful to supply the means for me to go on. I thought I had been abandoned by my brothers and sisters whom I had grown to love as we traveled to the place where I had to depart their company. I had felt betrayed by them, and perhaps by the Lord as well. I had become as a paralyzed man. I knew that I could not climb those heights without His help. Now I was assured that He had not forsaken me. He had sent this brother to help me when I could not hear well enough for myself to be encouraged by the Lord. There was so much to be learned upon the mountain.

Though I recovered greatly from my woundedness, I still felt somewhat abandoned and rejected for not being allowed to re-enter their company. I continued to deny that such a feeling was there, within me, but the evidence began to surface. It was first expressed in avoiding the stream. In doing so, I began to lead the people towards the deep forest rather than on the path by the stream. I hated the direction that I was taking them, but it was easier than facing the ugliness of what was in my heart. When beside the stream, I would always hear, though faintly, the melody which would tug on my heart to let go of the bitterness, for it did not belong there. I felt that it would be better dealt with later. I convinced myself that I was justified in my feelings, so I now went my own way. It grew dark within the forest as we continued the path that led across, not up, the mountain. Those whom I led were unaware, for the most part, that we were not pursuing the heights because they trusted me to lead them. I did not return to the stream but I did listen to the faint song carried on the wind. The wind seemed to be present all over the mountain, blowing in and out of the camps and even in the forest. Most people in the camps did not even acknowledge the wind because it was just a part of life on the mountain, but here I became keenly aware of it. It's melody and songs were not as distinct as the stream. I think it rather served to mention the stream, to call us to it. However, sometimes it blew with a mighty force. The wind was said to have even caused the destruction of some of the camps long ago. It remained present with us during our journey through the woods and I was glad that it did. I felt a responsibility for those who followed me, so I quite often searched the book that spoke of the mountain and the Lord of the mountain. I began to draw upon it for direction. I reasoned it's meaning with my own mind rather than asking the Lord as I used to do while sitting by the stream. My reasoning became the things I began to feed the people as we journeyed.

As we went on, the forest became more and more dense, growing even darker and causing us to become very unsettled. I was unaware that this bitterness within me was my enemy, leading me to abandon the path that led up the mountain. I still felt I was justified in my feelings and waited in hope that the Lord would come and clear up the whole misunderstanding. All the time we traveled, the wind's song urged me to turn and head back toward the stream. I knew it, but I would not turn back. Instead, I justified every step I took in the wrong direction. Traveling on into the darkness of the forest I finally knew that we were completely lost. I was faced with one tragedy after another. As I led them, my brothers and sisters were placed in danger as their ankles bled from the thorns we traveled through trying to find our way, yet still they trusted me to lead them on. I had not yet taught them how to listen by the stream for the songs meant for them from the Chief-Musician. I had only told them about the songs I had heard so that they had only me to direct them. Many were bruised from falling on the rough terrain and the whole thing became a survival effort, every man for himself. We had become a desperate lot to the point that some of the people even began to complain against me. However, rather than confess my bitterness to them, I would simply try to encourage them. I became so discouraged that I wanted to abandon them and go off by myself. I thought that we should all fend for ourselves, but I could not bring myself to say it. As we marched on, I realized that I could not bear the burden of these people any longer. Rather, I could not bear to see them suffer for what I had neglected. The Book, though a guide in some respects, did not impart the needed qualities of leadership. All this was not the will of the Lord, and I knew that I must be reconciled to Him.

At that point, I went a little beyond the people, fell on my knees and wept those pent-up tears of bitterness. I lifted my voice in loud cries to the Lord. Remembering a certain section of the Book of which I had shared with the people a short time ago, I turned to read of a garden called Gethsemane, and of a battle. It was a time when one man was humbled by the surrender of His will to the will of His Father. As I read, I began to weep with a sorrow that was welling up within me. The soft breeze became a wind sweeping through the trees towering over me. I heard the Lord calling me back to the stream. I began to weep in deep grief as the bitterness poured out of me in teardrops falling to the ground. Love began to flood into me replacing the bitterness as it was flushed out and away.

After a time, I stood upright feeling cleansed and charged to go the way of the Lord. Ready to run back to the others with the joyful news that we would return to the stream, I was overcome with the sounds of panic among my brothers and sisters. There were shouts and screams coming from their direction. As I started towards them, I saw the source of alarm. The forest was on fire and it was heading in the direction of the gathering. I quickly joined them. We grabbed all that we could and began running through the forest away from the flames. As we ran, the flames pursued us. While running, I wondered, why, why was the Lord allowing such a thing to happen now, just when I was seeing clearly what had befallen me and was willing to repent of my wickedness. Would He now destroy us? We ran keeping close together so that none would be left behind. When we had run for some distance, and were near to giving up from exhaustion, an unexpected rain came hard and fast. Within a few moments, we were all soaked to the bone. The smell of a dying fire filled our nostrils like a heavenly scent. Almost immediately, with one accord, we began lifting our faces towards the heavens allowing the rains to wash over us. Raising our voices with joy and gladness, we gave humble thanks for the miracle of deliverance we were receiving. Like children we fell to the muddy earth and laid there looking up to the clouds in silence. It was as if we all knew that no words were suitable enough to express our delight and amazement. The Lord had undoubtedly expressed His love for us in this wondrous event.

The rain slowed to a fine mist. We looked upward to see a rainbow crowning the top of the mountain. The memories that it stirred within me were sweet and exhilarating. As all gazed upon its beauty, I heard a familiar sound just over the knoll behind us. I ran to the top of the knoll to see if it was what I had suspected. There stretched out before me like a soothing bed, waiting for me to rest within its waters, was the comforting stream. Revelation flooded my mind. The fire had been given to drive us back to the place of blessing. We were lost in the darkness of the forest. Through the affliction of the flames, the Lord had led us back to the stream. My voice sounded like a trumpet as I called everyone to the stream. Our day of celebration was as great as any I had ever enjoyed. As evening approached I withdrew from my brothers and sisters and spent some time by myself to reflect on things. When I thought more about the battle in the garden, I began to see the tremendous struggle we all must face to deny ourselves and to follow the way of the Lord. I had been delighted to serve Him as long as I had seen it was to my advantage and it delighted my soul, but it was hard to go His way when it was so contrary to what I had wanted or expected from Him. It was so wonderful to receive from Him yet so hard to give back. I now realized that when I had entered the large camp I had begun to question Him in my heart and to resist Him. Subtly, fear and doubt began to replace the joy in serving Him. To some extent, anger and resentment choked the pleasure of loving Him and receiving love from Him. I knew I must somehow learn to overcome as did the one in the garden. It was said that He learned obedience through the things that He had suffered. I did not understand, but I then prayed that I could be taught. The first fire of His love within the camp transformed a people. This second fire of His love turned us from the way of destruction and back to the heights of glory. How strange, I thought, that the same love coming to us in the gentle melody of the stream and the soft soothing breeze, would also come to us in the burning heat of fire. And then the saving rains.

THE GARDEN

Gethsemane, your olive branches speak of peace,
A symbol of prosperity and blessing, of beauty and strength.
You are the crown that sits upon the heads of those who win the race.
You are named a garden, that which brings thoughts of beauty,
But I know you as a place of betrayal and agony.
You are hard on those who walk among your trees.
We do not smell the fragrance of your blossoms,
Neither is the shade from your branches any relief to us.
The trail which brings us here demands a price,
And we are all spent.
We are overcome, we are weak and sick of heart.

Who has led me to you Gethsemane?
I would not have come here on my own.
I have followed my Lord to your gate,
But now it seems He is gone.
How many have you been host to?
How many have endured the night in this place?
It is hard, Gethsemane to enter your gates,
But harder still to stay the night.
I have been this way before and thought you cruel,
And turned and went away, my way!
Now, once again I stand within your walls of green,
But still your blossoms do not yield a fragrance sweet.

Now, I am like a madman,
My thoughts are running wild.
I fear that I shall live to face this night,
And so, I want to die.
I fear that I shall die in darkness,
And so, I want to live.
I want to stay and find the morning star,
The hope of glory, rising in splendor
And lighting my way from here.
Yet, I want to run and leave this graveyard and my fear.
The hour grows late and I am all alone.
Your night is cold and lonely.
Where are they who traveled with me?
Have they not entered here as well?
Why do they not comfort me?
Will you deny me that as well, Gethsemane?
Why do you chasten me so harshly?
My flesh cries out with longing, and you despise me.
Reason escapes me and understanding is gone from me.
Gethsemane, you are without compassion.
Are you a robber of dreams?
A slayer of hopes?
You delight in death, for death is your purpose.
You feed upon the decay of dead desires.
How can I endure you?
I think that I cannot.
Once again, I must turn and go out from you.
I have failed you Gethsemane.
But, you have not failed me.
You have won.
I leave behind in you a carcass.

Feed upon it that your leaves may grow green.
For one day, I shall wear that crown made from your branches.

I have died a death that was long and hard,
But only the death found in failure.
Yet I know I must return again.
One day I shall enter your courts, and stay the night.
Then with torment past, and labors laid aside to save this life,
I shall lose it and ascend to heights unknown.
You shall have me again Gethsemane,
As your student, I shall kneel in your courts.
For He who leads me here has conquered you,
And I must, too.

CHAPTER SIX

THE NEW BEGINNING

I had been directed by the Lord to erect a new settlement upon the mountain. It seemed so contrary to what I thought was my calling of ascending the mountain. I believed that I had heard the Lord telling me that much needed to be learned before I could scale the high cliffs at the top of the mountain. I then began to build structures and direct those who were with me. Weeks turned into months, months turned into years, and things were going quite well, except that there seemed to be a loss of joy and excitement within the camp. Everything seemed to become routine and almost mundane.

Calling upon the Lord, I sought a way out of the camp's mundane, religious ritual of life, and a way into a standing before the Lord in real life and real fellowship. Once again, my life in the Lord had begun to wane, causing me to want to be awakened from my slumber into a renewed sense of destiny. I had to acknowledge that my years of giving a minimal amount of labor to the kingdom was eroding the joy of service. The kingdom, which is what the mountain was called, was itself slowly deteriorating through the increasing engagement with the invading sea. Those from the sea expanded their kingdom, from sea to shore, and then from the shore to the mountain. Day after day, I would make the same commitment to turn things around and really give myself to the things of the Lord. Once I ended conversing with the Lord and began my day out among the others, my commitment was always cast into the future. I was very aware of what was happening, as evidenced by the fact that my conversation with the Lord so often was, "Deliver me from evil, oh Lord; create within me a new heart and return to me the zeal that I once had for serving you." However, over and over again, I would determine, almost immediately upon making the request, that the effort was too great for any real change that day. Perhaps tomorrow I would start to fast and really seek the Lord and His destiny for me upon the mountain. Then, as tomorrow opened up, the cares of the world would once again choke out any earnest desire and lead to another repetitious promise. This promise I had made to myself, of course. I knew better than to promise the Lord that tomorrow I would begin my quest to turn things around and that I would become more kingdom-minded and less worldly. The tomorrows became weeks and the weeks became months. Now, years later, I was still looking for the day of new beginnings to actually dawn.

It seemed to me that my life had become almost nostalgic, like waiting for the spring rains to bring out the first buds on the trees as evidence of new life after a hard winter. I knew that hope was still alive within me, but there was no anticipation that evidenced real faith. I remembered what it had felt like to awaken each morning with the joy of the Lord welling up within me, excited for what the day would demonstrate about the reality of God. Presently, it was as if I was waking every morning just looking for some evidence of the rain and the promise of new life, but my sleepy eyes of faith had grown dim. Every once in a while, I would think back on my life and wonder why there were so many ups and downs. Why couldn't I maintain that flow of faithfulness? I began to understand that it was because I always wanted to be at that high level in my relationship with the Lord. I just couldn't settle for the valleys; I wanted the mountain top and beyond.

Another day had ended. I had fallen asleep after repeating the same nightly words, "Lord, be pleased to speak to me in a dream this night I pray." Most mornings I would awaken, arise, acknowledge the Lord, and begin my day. This particular morning when I awoke, something was different. I felt a stirring inside as I lay in the warmth of my bed. A smile came to my face as I felt surrounded by the love of the Lord. I could easily identify the feeling, because so often, during the tender years with the Lord, I would be wrapped in His embrace as He would shut out the world about me and make me to know a love so inviting that it blinded me to anything else. After a time of enjoying the moment and the memories that it stirred, I tried to reason out the *why* of it. I began to labor over the thought of why all of a sudden, like going to sleep in the darkness of a day's end and then awakening into the light of a new day, did I find myself awakened to the light of my Lord and the warmth of His love. The rain had come and new life was brought forth. But why? I had the evidence of new life, but when did it first spring up? It was as if something had infused me over night. As I thought about it, perhaps it had been developing within me for some time without recognition as my mind was trying to realize what was happening. I lay there in outward silence, but within began the gathering of words that would produce a sentence and the gathering of thought that would produce a direction resulting in a renewed determination. It was like a sprout pushing up through the ground's soil moistened by the new rain. This new determination was that the kingdom of the Lord must advance within me and that this new life must be further watered and nourished. The thoughts were racing through my head and producing such an excitement that I threw back the blankets and stood to my feet and then headed downstairs to give myself to fellowship with the Lord. This was truly a new day.

I couldn't help but be amazed at how the Lord works so quietly within the soul of a man, until the yielding that He desires actually takes place. I really could own no part of the new state of joy I found to be within. Aside from the half-hearted desire that produced the lame effort towards a new beginning, I had done nothing. No, this was all the Lord's doing. The Lord had drawn me once again to Himself. All that the following days would bring would be solely authored by the Lord. It was as if the flood gates of heaven had been opened and I was dreaming dreams, seeing visions, enjoying an ongoing conversation with my Lord, and delighting in it all. I had been awakened from my slumber and the new beginning was finally at hand. During my conversations with the Lord, He recalled to me the same words that had been given by the stream some years ago:

Look higher than the mountains,
Don't' cast your eyes towards ground,
Seek to pierce the clouds on high,
With gaze towards heaven now be found.
Don't stop at lofty peaks to dwell,
Where man can climb and victory tell,

But, long to soar beyond man's means,
To places formed for God's redeemed.
Look higher than the mountains,
To where the flowing stream begins,
The source is not in snow-capped peaks
It has it's start where all things end.

I determined to reconsider these words, spoken to me so long ago, in the light of this new day. After all, they contained a call that I knew was tied to my destiny in the Lord. One night, I spoke the usual words that ended my day, "Be pleased my Lord to speak to me in a dream tonight". In a melodic stream running through my mind, the familiar words flowed, "Look higher than the mountains..." They ran through my mind over and over again, until the words took me into a slumber, followed by a deep sleep where a dream would then define these words with theatrical movement.

As I slept, I dreamed of the mountain again. The whole mountain was full of activity within the various camps. It became clear that upon the mountain there was a great upheaval. Change was being called for as men had come up from the sea with new ways, new words, and reports of fantastic things. After hearing of these astonishing things many within the camps wanted to move away from the mountain and the stream and down to the sea. Others within the camps were inviting those from the sea to bring the ways of the sea into the mountain. Those who were opposed to these changes, because they believed these new ways to violate the old ways and traditions, were forced out of the camps. As these exiles began to ascend to the top of the mountain, they were accompanied by others.

Awakening in the morning, I began to ponder these things and to call upon the Lord for revelation concerning them. I knew that within the dream were things that concerned my destiny. I could distinguish that there was a call to something higher, something greater than I could verbalize at that present time. I had to be content to allow these things to unfold in their own time, nonetheless, I also prayed and sought the Lord for understanding.

Once again, I considered the amazing ways of the Lord. Somehow, I had been given a dream in which I was aware that I was in a dream. While in the dream, I saw a vision and was given knowledge of events occurring upon the mountain within the kingdom of God, in the earth. Words that I had read in the Book flooded my mind, and I began to wonder at the possibilities of man, created in the image and likeness of his Creator. What if the man in the garden had not sinned? What if man had been free to be who he was created to be without the death that sin had brought? What was the full potential of man when free to be truly united to God? This whole experience filled me with wonder. I knew that this dream was somehow linked to the reality of this world and the kingdom of God within it. I desired to know the meaning, but also understood that I must wait upon the Lord who was the only one who could rightly disclose the meaning. Attention must be paid to the seemingly little things in life when one is endeavoring to discern to what it is that the Lord would call him. I must keep in mind, I thought, that there are two realities to be considered, the spiritual and the natural. To find one's destiny is to yield one's life to the urging and leading of the one who brings the songs, who alone can give to us the spiritual significance of the events in our lives. If our life is to be found in Him, then we must often sit by the steam and listen for the song. We must be able to connect one event to another in order to gain ground. We must understand that there are no isolated events in our lives, that each event is somehow related to others.

I decided to enter into a time of fasting to draw near to the Lord. During this time of fasting, though the body becomes weary, the heart is more fully given to the Lord and the spirit becomes more sensitive to the voice of the Holy One. At one point during this fast I was praying and the Lord began to speak to me of the dream I had been given. The dream began to flood my mind as if I were living it and as I listened to the Lord who began to interpret it, I began to understand the meaning. He showed me that the mountain represented the kingdom. The stream and the songs from the stream flowed from His throne to direct the people within the camps. Each of the camps represented the various parts of the whole kingdom. The stream flowing down through the mountain represented the flow of the Holy Spirit as did the wind and the fire. The tree at the bottom of the mountain between the sea and the mountain represented the place of rebirth for all who had come to the truth of salvation in the Lord, the Tree of Life. It was both the tree on which He hung and the Tree of Life. Each individual who was born again would begin his ascent to the top of the mountain, being nourished by the stream and by each camp's knowledge and practice of the truths of God. The sea represented unredeemed humanity. It was from this sea of humanity that the disturbance upon the mountain originated. Those leaving the camps in protest of these new things coming up from the sea of humanity were the remnant of God who were being called up higher, so as not to enter into the compromise coming into the camps from the sea. As I pondered these things, I knew that there would be more understanding to come. While considering this, the word came to me once again, adding more meaning to not only the visions, but the call, "Look higher than the mountains . . ."

CHAPTER SEVEN

THE INDIVIDUAL
AND THE COLLECTIVE

I began spending more and more time apart from the others and studying the Book that spoke of the mountain, especially focusing on those who had traveled to the mountain long ago. One of the things that struck me was the telling of a young man who began by tending his father's sheep. This lad, known as David, was the youngest of eight sons. I began to see something in his life that intrigued me so I began to study his life. I found that it was very prophetic of his destiny that, as a boy, he would be a shepherd watching over his father's sheep. In the years to come he would be called by the Lord to be king over Israel, a shepherd of the people of God. That was even prophetic of his future descendant who would come to the mountain to save those upon the mountain and He would be called the Shepherd of His people Israel. I began to pray about what the Lord would teach me about my own life. Could David's life speak to me about my destiny? Two things began to occupy my mind during times of meditation. First, it was the reality of the personal destiny for David while being a part of the whole house of Israel. It was so apparent to me that within the framework of the camps many people of God were not looking for any personal destiny. They were content to follow the crowd, to be a part of the whole without any individual sense of destiny. David was obviously busy about the affairs of the kingdom upon the mountain, but he would often draw himself away to spend time with the Lord and would write songs or psalms concerning the things that he heard and saw from the Lord. He was said to have a heart after God. The songs that the Lord, the Chief-Musician, would give to him would take him far beyond his own personal destiny in this world. He truly communed with the Lord of the mountain. I looked at my life upon the mountain and could see that I must be a destiny seeker. I would seek my destiny in Him and encourage others to do the same. If we could all find our individual destinies, I was sure that we could find them fitting together with the others without diminishing our own walk before Him. This would require setting aside time to be with Him just as David did and just as the Shepherd of Israel had done during His time upon the mountain. He too would withdraw and seek His destiny and how to fulfill it before His Father, the One who dwells on high.

I also was suddenly engaged with this people called Israel. The Book was full of references to them being the people of God, being in covenant with God, being given their own destiny as a people and being the "apple of His eye". Where were they? What had happened to them? So, I began to study the origin and history of this people. What I found amazed me. It was as if I had been walking with a candle to light my way and now a flood light had been turned on. The whole Book that I had been studying became light and life for me. Once again, a vision was given to me. I was drawn to this ancient path upon the mountain and walking this path within a vision.

As I watched myself walk upon this path it took me someplace I had never been before. It took me to the other side of the mountain. What I saw on the other side of the mountain was this nation called Israel. They had always been on the mountain but somehow separated from sight. I couldn't contain myself. I shouted with joy and knew for certain that my destiny would lead me here and somehow, I would be joined with this Israel of God. I would study their heritage, learn from David and from those called the fathers. I would share with my companions all that I had seen and hope that, as was so often the case, the Holy Spirit would go before me to prepare the way within their hearts. However, I had one thing that I needed to do first. I had to get a second witness. I watched for the Lord to bring to me this second witness before proceeding any further.

As I shared with my companions the love that the Lord of the mountain had for Israel, we also began to love Israel. We began to pray for whatever the Lord was doing on the other side of the mountain with Israel. We began to feel a kinship with Israel, though we had no real connection with them upon the mountain. It was during this time of praying for Israel that we were given an understanding of a great truth in the Book. An apostle of the Lord, named Paul, wrote about Israel. He had traveled both sides of the mountain and he was given to understand this great truth and it was in his destiny to teach this truth. He explained that we do have a real connection with Israel. We are in fact, grafted into Israel and that without this relationship to Israel through faith in the Lord of the mountain we could not complete our climb. Rather than being disappointed by this truth, we were elated. So many things would make sense now. Things, that before, we could not understand were clear. We knew that we would meet

Israel at the top of the mountain and that we would together enter that place formed for God's redeemed. We would find the true fathers of our faith there. We would find the Lord of the mountain there.

CHAPTER EIGHT

THE HOLY CONVERSATION

Once again, while meditating on the things of the Lord, I began expressing my gratitude to God for the way the Holy Spirit had been ministering to me of late. That sense of destiny continued to grow within me; however, I was not free of the trials and tribulations encountered in everyday life. The accelerated pace on the mountain was still bearing down upon me seeking to distract me from the things of the Kingdom. As I was bemoaning those things that I had allowed to distract me, I recognized that the dream concerning the mountain not only represented things external to me, but also things internal: the mountain was within me as well. The way was in me, the stream was in me, I was my own camp, and there was that sea of humanity always trying to find inroads into my camp, into my soul. I, too, had to be on guard against the compromise that the kingdoms of this world would utilize to become a part of my camp, a part of my life. I determined within my own heart to ascend the mountain, the calling of God within. If I was to continue to ascend, I had to fix my eyes on the Lord, the author and perfector of my faith. I recalled the words of my Lord, "For indeed, the kingdom of God is within you."

I knew there was still so much to learn about being in the world and yet not of the world. I also knew all my difficulties were used to test my faith so that the word of God within me could be proven, and thus God be glorified. It was not that the Lord brought trials and tribulations to me, but that the Lord used the trials and tribulations I encountered upon the mountain to test and thereby strengthen my faith in the word of God. The Lord's brother, James, understood this to be the way of the Lord, "My brethren, count it all joy when you fall into various trials, knowing that the testing of your faith produces patience. But let patience have its perfect work, that you may be perfect and complete, lacking in nothing" (James 1: 2–4). Perfect and complete. I knew I was far from that, and if it were trials that produced this outcome, then I knew I was in for quite a journey. I wondered if I could endure. Quickly, the Holy Spirit came with the word of another disciple to comfort me. "He who calls you is faithful, who also will do it" (1 Thess. 5:24). I thanked God and vowed to myself that I would move into the days ahead with a solid conviction and a very sober determination.

A great deal had been exchanged during my time with the Lord that day. After the exchange, there were two words that lingered in my mind. Those two words were contained with a command, "Tell my people that I want them to enter into a holy conversation." The two words within that command, that I continued to mull over, were "holy conversation". What was a holy conversation, I wondered. One could speculate as to the meaning, but it seemed so obvious what that speculation would produce that I reasoned there must be more to it than that. Was the Lord speaking about a single conversation or an ongoing conversation? Was I to initiate that conversation, or would I just recognize it when I was engaged in it? With whom would I be engaged? Was the holy conversation to be between me and the people, between the people and the Lord, or between me and the people about the Lord?

I considered these things for several weeks. The Holy Spirit had said, "Tell My people that I want them to enter into a holy conversation." I knew that once these words came out of my mouth that I would have to answer the questions that I myself had posed. This command and the questions about it were to work deep within me and ultimately out through me unto those with whom I walked and who, therefore, shared in my destiny and I in theirs. However, I sensed the need, even before these words were fully worked within me, to cast them out before my companions and let the conversation begin. I wondered though, would this initiate the *holy conversation*, or would it bring confusion? Certainly, a holy conversation could not begin with confusion. I was concerned that I would bring something into the camp that would separate the people, like those who came up from the sea had done in my dream. But, these words were not from the sea of humanity, they were not born out of the philosophies of men, they came from the Lord, if indeed I had heard correctly. Then I began to wonder if perhaps the camp to which I belonged might already have been polluted, and whether these dreams, and words were being given to clear out that pollution. Perhaps there was deception in the camp already. After all, the nature of deception is that you don't know that you are deceived. Had our camp been polluted by those who had come in from the sea, from the world, with worldly expressions? Was this command for a holy conversation to clarify and distinguish the truth of God from compromise? I wished the Lord would communicate in a more, straight forward manner. If only things could be made clearer. But then it struck me, it was to be a walk of faith. I had to trust in the Lord and in my relationship with the Lord and be obedient to Him who is faithful and true. As those thoughts entered my mind, I recognized that faithful companion once again, reminding me of what the Lord had promised.

"However, when He, the Spirit of truth, has come, He will guide you into all truth; for He will not speak on His own authority, but whatever He hears He will speak [. . .] He will take of what is Mine and declare it to you" (John 16:13–14).

I would find that these two words would significantly alter the course of my life and, by the power of the Holy Spirit, would begin to cause a separation within my own being and within those who traveled with me. Those two words, "holy conversation", cast forth in the Spirit of God would be living words, powerful and sharp, and would pierce even to the division of soul and spirit within the hearers of the words. The spirit of each man and woman who would hear these words and would receive them into their regenerated spirits, would begin to face the battle, which the unregenerate soulish part within each of them would require them to enter. This battle would be a fight for the direction they would take. After hearing these words, they would experience the pulling and tugging of an internal struggle, while striving to enter into and remain in that holy conversation. The battle within would take on the same nature as that which the Apostle Paul spoke of within himself, in his letter to the Church of Rome. He said, "For I delight in the law of God according to the inward man. But I see another law in my members, warring against the law of my mind, and bringing me into captivity to the law of sin which is in my members" (Rom. 7:22–23). I believed that my brothers and sisters in the Lord would delight in the word of God according to the inward man that was infused with the Spirit of God. I had found them to be sensitive to the Holy Spirit and to judge things well. However, they would see another law in their members, warring against the law of their minds, and bringing them into captivity to the law of sin, which is in our members, that Adamic nature, the unregenerate part of man. They would find that the flesh did not enjoy indulging in the holy conversation. The flesh enjoyed indulging in the lust of the flesh, the lust of the eyes and the boastful pride of life, none of which leads to a holy conversation. The battle would be real. The victory over the flesh could only come through yielding to the Holy Spirit within this holy conversation.

These two words, "holy conversation", would become a discerner of the thoughts and intentions of the heart, and cause a conflict that would drive toward surrender or resistance. One choice would produce life and peace in the inward man, and the other only death and greater conflict. Every conversation would be challenged and measured by the standard of holiness. Were they speaking of the things of God or speaking only foolishness? Is the conversation edifying or discouraging, pure or vile, challenging and uplifting or judgmental and condemning? Above all, was the truth of God the standard by which they would judge what was being stated, both upon the mountain and in the world?

Words that are brought from the throne of God to the camps and words that are born out of a conversation with God, carry with them the transforming and sanctifying power of God. These words then become the prophetic voice of the mountain. This powerful work is all contained within the ongoing holy conversation with God and among His people. It is only this prophetic voice that demands the word of God be brought forth to purify the mountain. It is then, in turn, only the prophetic voice that can challenge the world in the power of the Holy Spirit. This prophetic voice brings life to the people who live upon the mountain and denies a pathway into their lives for the philosophies of men which challenge the very word of God. I believed in the power of the prophetic word of God and I committed myself to the cause I believed my Lord was commissioning me to walk out.

I soon discovered I was not the only one who was being nudged by the Holy Spirit to step back from the world and engage more with the Kingdom of God. Once I had spoken the word, I found that it was a collective call to change direction. Others had been hearing similar things and together they rejoiced, giving thanks for the witness of two or three establishing the voice of the Holy Spirit in the midst of them. The Holy Spirit had gone before me and had prepared the way for the word of the Lord. Once again, I could own none of it, because it was the Holy Spirit that had prepared them to hear and respond to the call for a holy conversation. Oh, how amazing are His works within the hearts of men and how wondrous are His ways to accomplish them, I thought. With that thought, I gave thanks in humble adoration to the God of love.

CHAPTER NINE

THE ANCIENT PATHS

Throughout the next few weeks and months I, along with others began to look beyond the confines of our dwelling. We could see that this stirring by the Holy Spirit was taking place all throughout the camps upon the mountain. We could also see a division taking place upon the mountain. Those who were bringing forth a similar message of a prophetic call to a return to the truth, to a holy conversation were undergoing tremendous criticism from the world around them. As the compromise within the camps was being exposed by the prophetic call, surprisingly it was being defended by many within the camps and causing much discord. It was as the dream had demonstrated. Many were leaving their camps and pursuing the higher peaks upon the mountain. The criticism directed towards them was coming as much from within the camps as from without.

It was not long before another two words given to us by the Holy Spirit were added to the holy conversation. These two words were "ancient paths". This was not a call to simply know of the ancient paths, because we had known of them. This was a call to understand what the ancient paths were. I thought this could be much like the earlier awakening within the camps, which was a call to be empowered by the Holy Spirit through

His gifting to those upon the mountain. That call, which I had answered and entered into at the foot of the mountain, was also condemned by some on the mountain and mocked by the world. That same call had led me and so many others to ascend the mountain. Then there seemed to be a straying from the path as men built doctrines pertaining to that move of the Holy Spirit. These were doctrines that once again brought a mixed worship upon the mountain. It was a mixed form of worship such as once took place with a king named Ahab and the people he ruled in the name of God. It was a mixed form of worship that had to be addressed by the Apostle Paul. Now, there was a mixed form of worship upon the mountain crafted in a way that disguised the reality of what it truly was. There was now a need to call the camps back to these ancient paths and a need to understand what these paths were. Why? Because, our Lord Himself had said, "Enter by the narrow gate, for wide is the gate and broad is the way that leads to destruction, and there are many who go in by it. Because narrow is the gate and difficult is the way which leads to life, and there are few who find it" (Matt. 7:13–14). The way leading to life was to be found upon the ancient paths.

I decided to study the book concerning this issue of mixed worship. I found that the prophet Elijah had been sent to King Ahab, who had allowed an idol to be set up in the temple of God and that this mixed worship had angered the Lord. The message of Elijah then was to address this mixed worship and the ministry of Elijah was to set things straight according to the way the Lord desired to be worshiped. John the Baptist was then sent in the spirit and power of Elijah to address this same issue of mixed worship. The religious community of John's day had mixed man made traditions with the instruction from God. He was calling them back to a pure form of worship. Worship was to be in sprit and in truth. I wondered with this call for a holy conversation, and with so many hearing it, if it would result in the ministry of Elijah going forth once again preparing for the return of the Lord to the mountain. The holy conversation would include a return to the ancient paths separating from any form of mixed worship and heading back to the mountain, seeking to climb its peaks and await the return of the Lord.

Another dream had entered my sleep. It was a dream that would awaken me to a change that was taking place in both realms of reality: the spiritual and the physical. Within the dream was a banquet table that extended as far as I could see to the west. Seated on both sides of the table were men and women who were all clothed in robes and the table was full of what appeared to be fine foods. I too was seated at this table. We were all eating from what was on the table and were quite happy and content. Then, suddenly from the east, came a figure. He was dressed in a white robe and, as He closed the distance between us, His identity became known to me. It was the Lord of the mountain. He approached and then called out to me and said, "The time for this banquet is over. Stand, shake the crumbs from your garments and follow Me; change is coming to the mountain."

I considered this dream for several days, prayed about its meaning, considered it in light of the Book, the written Word of God, and in light of current world events, which I had been watching with an interest believing them to be relevant to the prophetic times in which we were living. With great sadness, I also could see that the camps upon the mountain were the concern of the dream. I then related the dream to a few of my companions and it was determined that it should become a subject within the holy conversation, hoping that its meaning could be more fully clarified and understood. Throughout the conversation about the dream, there was agreement that the Lord was calling those who would follow Him away from the table. Had it somehow been compromised? Stand up and shake the crumbs from your garments! What did that mean? Leave no trace of it upon your soul? Certainly, if this table represented the camps at large and the food upon it was compromised, though it looked good and most were still eating from it, then it appeared to them to be in keeping with the previous dream about the mountain. Surely the Lord was calling for some kind of separation: a separation from something and a call to something else. It seemed to most that the table must be the spiritual food that they had been partaking of, but why were they to be separated from that sustenance? I thought of the adage, "you are what you eat". Perhaps if we begin to examine who we were, we would find the answer. We began to counsel together concerning these things and how the dream and the ancient paths might relate to each other. Within the counsel of this conclave one stood and urged all to consider what the Holy Spirit might be saying about the ancient paths. Were we being called to something new or to return to something old? Perhaps we were being urged to return to a place that had been forgotten, the ancient paths. There was a real sense among all who had engaged in this conversation that something was about to break forth. There was now, the holy conversation, the ancient paths, and the call to leave something to follow the Lord as He lead us to a "new way". This new way may have been leading back to the old ways, back to the ancient paths. Was the new way the ancient paths? Did all these things fit together?

As we studied the scriptures together concerning these things, we discovered that these paths were ancient, but not old in the sense of being out dated. As we studied the Word of God, it became clear to all that these ancient paths ran throughout the history of God's dealings with man. The ancient paths were intended to be carried into the present and prophetically were in sight right up to the consummation of all things. A new path was never given by the Lord. An alternate way was never to replace the way He had inaugurated. The word "everlasting" kept coming up in our study of these things. We concluded that what the Holy Spirit was leading us to understand was that what was forgotten had been lost and what was lost had to be restored. The new way that we were to follow was actually the old way, the ancient paths, established before the foundation of the world. Contained within these ancient paths were the creative words of God that brought into being the worlds and light and life. These paths began at the very throne of God and extended from there, out into the created universe which is sustained by its attachment to His throne. These ancient paths led from the throne of God to the garden of Eden as a path upon which Adam and Eve stood with the Lord of all creation in unbroken fellowship. The paths led out of the garden after Adam and Eve's rebellion against their Creator and became paths laden with the love and grace of God for His fallen creation. They then became known as the way of salvation established upon the promise of restoration. "[. . .] He shall bruise your head, and you shall bruise His heel" (Gen. 3:15). Abraham walked upon these paths, Moses walked upon these paths, Samuel walked upon these paths, David walked upon these paths, and all the prophets walked upon these paths as did God's people, when they were obedient to Him. Their disobedience had been in straying from these paths where upon they could know blessing and protection. They were continually called back to these paths by a loving God. The Lord Himself stayed on these paths throughout His earthly life. He also taught His disciples to walk in the ancient paths and explained to them what they were. These were the paths of covenant and they had been compromised by the camps upon the mountain. We had strayed from the ancient paths while forging our own paths, seeking to sanctify the traditions of man rather than holding to the sanctity of God's way, the ancient paths.

The people who were now hearing the calling of God to return to these ancient paths were beginning to understand that the camps had left the ancient paths. The camps had compromised the truth, had polluted the way, had forsaken the holy for the profane, and had made alliances with the world. They had replaced the wisdom of God with the so-called wisdom of this world. The philosophies of men had unseated the theology of God as the queen of the academic disciplines. Man, by his own assertion, had "come of age" and wisdom was to be found in his own reasoning. These were the things being brought to the mountain by those upon the sea. Rather than learn from the revelation that was to be unfolded within the pages of the Word of God, line upon line, precept upon precept, man would add his own collective knowledge. Science, the knowledge of the physical world, psychology, man's understanding of man, and the great increase of technology would so impress those within the camps that they would contend that there must be a compromise of reason and faith. They sought an equal footing between God and man in order for there to be any need found for the mountain and the camps in this age of modernity. Once these thoughts flooded my mind, I fell on my face before God and cried out, "Oh God, deliver your people from this evil that has come upon us. Forgive us for forsaking your truth". I thought of what the Lord had said to the prophet Daniel concerning the last days, "But you, Daniel, shut up the words, and seal the book until the time of the end; many shall run to and fro, and knowledge shall increase" (Dan. 12:4). "Many shall be purified, made white, and refined, but the wicked shall do wickedly; and none of the wicked shall understand, but the wise shall understand" (Dan. 12:10). Were we in these last days? Was the knowledge of the ancient paths that which would purify and make white?

All of these grand issues that seemed as big as the world in which we lived were now very concerning to these few and seemingly insignificant people within the camp where we dwelled. We understood that we were a part of the mountain and we believed that we had heard from the Lord of the mountain. And so, we prayed and humbled ourselves, gathering around what we believed to be the leading of the Lord. We endeavored to hold to a holy conversation and to follow the Lord's leading as He disclosed to us the ancient paths. We recognized that, as the dream had so vividly displayed, the table that we had once gathered around was no longer the table of the Lord. It had been compromised.

Understanding that the holy conversation was to be kept foremost in our minds and that we had to battle to root out other distractions by taking captive every thought to the obedience of our Lord, we determined to remain alert to the call. The dream brought to us the awareness that not only were we being called to something, but we were also being called from something: a table that no longer provided for us what God demanded. Evidently, it was time to rise up from the table and to set out on a course to be forged by the Lord Himself. It was from this awareness that a question arose. Was God once again calling forth a remnant? All throughout the ages, God had kept for Himself a remnant which would not bend the knee to the false gods of the world and which would not compromise the truth of God and which would not leave the ancient paths. Were we hearing that call? Could we trust what we were hearing? Here was one more consideration to be added and judged within the holy conversation.

During the holy conversation, we not only considered what the ancient paths might be, but how it was that we had forgotten them. In order to forget something, one must formerly have known of it. Did we only know of it and never really walk upon these paths or did we once walk upon them and not realize our departure from them? No one seemed to know quite how to answer that, though we were not lacking in conjecture. I thought that I had been walking on the path of the Lord from the beginning at the foot of the mountain. Had I become confused during my stay within some of the camps? The one thing that had become clear with an almost unanimous consensus was that everything up until now had to do with walking through this life viewing everything from God's perspective and that is what we endeavored to do. Man's perspective was so often short sighted and indifferent to the very Word of God. His perspective is what we desired, allowing His word to interrupt His word.

The kingdom of God and the camps within that kingdom had to have distinction from the kingdoms of this world and it seemed that the lines had become blurred. It seemed that something had gone terribly wrong. The mountain was supposed to influence the world with the good news of

salvation and the ways of the Lord, the way of salvation to a
lost world. Instead, it appeared that the world was influencing
many of the camps with its ways. The mountain was to stand
tall as the conscience of society and yet it appeared that society
had substantially quieted the voice from the mountain. All
within the conversation agreed that the world was a very
unsettling place for most of them. We agreed that we could
easily understand how many things could have been forgotten
and lost as the pace of life around us had accelerated us into a
world so inundated with the increase in technology. Modernity
seemed to make the mountain obsolete for much of the world.
We agreed that the camps seemed to feel the need to be more
attentive to the things of the world or lose their place in it.
There seemed to be a certain fear of being left behind and a
fear of no longer being relevant to the society in which we
existed. But, then this call was sounded. This was a call to halt
our progression within that world and to return to the ancient
paths. If we were to heed this call, then the decision had to
be made, the adjustments had to begin, and determination to
hold true had be strengthened. We all agreed the call was good,
but none the less it was, to say the least, very unsettling.

The holy conversation had begun and it would be a
conversation about everything in life, a kind of resubmitting
to old, basic foundational truths and letting those truths
determine what part within each individual belonged to this
world or the world that contained the ancient paths. Heart
and head, soul and spirit would be engaged in these holy
conversations and each conversation would become a part of a
stream of conversations that would become known as the holy
conversation of the way. The questions that would be asked
along the way would be many and complex and the challenge

would be to make the complex simple and easily understood by all who desired to walk together and in unison. We were to be of one mind along these paths.

What had brought us to the conclusion that there must be a separation between this modern world and the world to which the ancient paths belonged was simply the term "ancient". How could something ancient belong to the modern world? If indeed we were being called form one thing to another, was it from the modern world to the world of which these ancient paths belonged? Within the holy conversation that question was easily and quickly answered. Once again it was recalled that the Lord Himself had spoken of the difference between the kingdoms of this world and the Kingdom of God, which existed in this world, but was not to be "of the world". The paths of the Lord, though they be called ancient or modern, have never belonged to this world and its kingdoms. The paths of the Lord belonged to His kingdom, to the kingdom of heaven and those who walk upon them recognize that they are but sojourners in this world. Our association with this world is to be as ambassadors of the kingdom of God and never as agents of compromise with the world. We were to be ministers of reconciliation based upon the covenant of God with His people and never outside the covenant. We recognized that the light of this world may shine in darkness as men who desire good do good, but only the light of the Lord could extinguish darkness. Above all, it was not the role of the camps to make this good news relevant to this modern world. The word of God, the good news, the way of salvation for a lost world, has always been relevant and just. It is the task of God's people to make this truth known in their time. It is the task of the camps to make it known in our time, not through a cleverly devised relevant message, but through teaching the truths of the Lord, using His words. The ancient paths have forged their way through the rise and fall of many civilizations throughout the history of this world and their truth remains relevant, because it is the living and active word of God.

We had determined that we would leave the camp and pursue a way upon the ancient paths. We would hold to that which we deemed good, that which we had learned upon the mountain and within the other camps. We would seek to discern that which seemed consistent with the book, but we would reach out for that which the Lord of the mountain held before us. And so, we ascended the mountain remaining upon the ancient paths and looking for those places formed for God's redeemed.

PART II
MIRACLES AND REVELATIONS

CHAPTER TEN

THE REALITY

This allegory is, in fact, my personal experience with the Lord from the time I was born again up until this day. Before I was born into His kingdom, I was that discouraged and hopeless young man sitting at the window on the beach. Coming to know Christ and receiving His Holy Spirit, being reborn, as typified by the Tree of Life experience at the foot of the mountain, was the most meaningful and wonderful experience I have ever known. All the dreams and visions in the allegory were actually given to me by the Lord throughout my walk with Him. All of them had real life meaning and had to be walked out before Him and with those that He had given me to walk with. These dreams and visions guided my walk with Him throughout the last forty-three years. He has always spoken to me most directly through His living Word, but also through dreams and visions. Those whom He has given me to walk with through the years can attest to these dreams and visions. They not only stood by me to see these dreams and visions confirmed as having come from the Lord, but they also aided in walking out the direction that each has given to me. The first church that I pastored was called Fire of Love Christian Community Church. It was named that because of the first dream of the church exploding into flames after the people had entered in.

The building that had burst into flames in my dream was the traditional Catholic Church that I grew up attending. I had not attended that church since my youth. I went through a period of rebellion and began to reap the things I had sown in my rebellion and found myself in deep despair. I began crying out to God in that despair and asking Him to save my life, meaning to change it or to end it. Not long after I began pleading with the Lord, a knock on my door and the testimony of a man who had been sent to me began the change I had been praying for. When I received the Holy Spirit through the laying on of hands in a non-denominational, charismatic church, I remained with them for three years. It was at that point that the Lord directed me back to that same Catholic church through the dream. A new young priest had come to town and through a divine appointment I met him and that is who the Lord led me to share my dream with. I didn't know that he was looking for the Lord to send him someone to work with him in starting a charismatic group in that church. That is when the dream began to take on reality and I began to walk it out with this priest and about sixty of his parishioners. Through the course of the previous three years I had experienced a great move of the Holy Spirit in my life and in the life of the charismatic church I was attending. It became apparent to me that the priest had experienced very little of the moving of the Spirit. He pretty much let me take the lead in teaching and worship, while he continued to minister the sacraments. We worked well together for some time until it became evident that the Lord was leading me out of that church. A series of incidents that had taken place made it quite clear that it was time for my departure. I thought I would be returning home to the charismatic church that I had attended previously. Much to my surprise, about thirty of the parishioners wanted to leave the Catholic church with me. I resisted that move and went for counsel with the elders of the charismatic church I wanted to return to. They prayed for direction and determined that the Lord was directing me to begin to pastor these people with whom I had developed a relationship with over the three years of teaching and ministering to them. The elders had determined to ordain me and to help oversee the new church which would be called Fire of Love.

The night that I was ordained to the ministry, a little old prophet known as Brother Henry laid his hands on me and said, "Thus says the Lord, 'Jacob thou worm, I will thrash the mountain with you'". I latter found a passage that read "Fear not, you worm Jacob" (Isa. 41:14). I was very humbled by those words and often thought back on them during my weakest moments. What they spoke to me was that no matter how weak I was, He would take me in His hands and "thrash the mountain" with me. He would thrash every mountain that I faced and felt too big to conquer. He would be faithful to lead and guide me through all the falsehood that I would put my hand to in seeking His truth. He would tell me what I must pick up and hold to, and what I must lay aside. In my weaknesses, He would be my strength. This was important for me to learn because there would be so many times that I would find the weak and desperate within the kingdom. I would understand their fears and their weaknesses, because of my own. He would allow me to serve them in their weakness, directing them into the way of surrender that He had taught me and allowing me to be used by Him to thrash their mountains.

I have watched the church at large through the years go from being a stronghold of truth to compromising so much that it has lost much of its voice. A voice that once was as the Saviors song of hope to a wicked, perverse, and desperate world, had become almost silent and was standing on the sidelines of world events. I saw the compromise of others and rather than confront it, I allowed it to grant me permission to compromise as well. I saw this as my weakness, until He took hold of me over and over again to awaken me to the fact that I was embracing a reality that was not in accordance with His will. I was willing to walk in that compromise and even defend it. How faithful He has been throughout my life. How amazing is His love, His mercy, and His grace? Through this search for truth, He led me back to the beginning, to a search for our roots.

CHAPTER ELEVEN

THE KNOWLEDGE
AND THE THREAT

We had been planning a holy convocation. It was the beginning of spring and we had just come out of a hard winter. I believed that I had heard the Lord call for a time of separation and I knew that a holy convocation was a time for setting the people apart, a time for drawing close to Him. The convocation was to be in the fall and there was much to do in the way of planning, inviting guest speakers, and securing the location. Most of all, though I believed that I had heard the Lord tell me to plan for this convocation, I wasn't settled on the theme for it. We didn't want to just cast out a theme, we wanted to hear from the Lord. A separation from or to what specifically? This was something that I had been praying about and I believed that I had an idea of what the Lord would have the focus of the event to be; however, I felt that I still lacked that defining word. Therefore, I determined to call for a weekend of fasting and prayer; a kind of shut in for the men within the church.

The weekend was going well and there were several key men there whom I had asked to attend. We had begun to fast Friday morning and that evening we prayed through the night, some grabbing a few minutes of sleep here and there. We would pray together and then have a discussion concerning what we believed the Lord to be saying to us as individuals and then separate. We continued to pray, coming together again as someone called for another discussion believing some revelation had been given to him. This continued through Saturday and into that evening. During one of the times of corporate prayer late Saturday evening, a prophetic word came forth from me. It was a very sobering word of warning that the church must be very sober minded in these last days and that there was a separation coming that God was orchestrating by His Holy Spirit. The word spoke of a compromise that had come into the church, a compromise of His truth. That's when the theme of the last days opened up to us. The word I was given was calling for watchmen who would be faithful to declare the things that were to come to pass in the days ahead. After the word was shared with the men, we began to look to the scriptures concerning the prophetic message about the last days. One after the another, the men began to share from the Word and collectively we began to share an awareness that something of great significance had just been given to us. We continued to pray and ask the Lord to seal these things with a witness and to guide us in this course if it were indeed He who was directing us.

Since there was to be a gathering in the morning, we decided that it would be best if we all got some sleep. Having attended several men's retreats through the years and forced to lay silently awake aside the roar of snoring men, I laid claim to the nursery for my slumber. It was well carpeted, warm and above all, it was sound proof. The men all headed off to their different lairs and the lights went out. I was almost asleep when I heard the threatening voice. "If you continue on with this I will kill you." Right then a sharp pain in my chest, and then another. I began to call upon the name of the Lord, trying to calm myself and recalling those assuring passages from the Word of God about the Lord's protection and for a moment things seemed okay, but then another pain, this time causing me to sit directly up. I quickly got to my feet and turned the light on and then went to gather the men. I called out and the men came quickly to see what was going on. We regathered into the circle where we had been praying and I told them what had just happened. The men immediately laid hands on me and began to pray, rebuking the enemy and calling upon the Lord for protection. There was little discussion about the event, because no one really knew what to make of it. We all determined that the devil was just trying his fear tactics and that he was a liar. After a short time, I assured them that I was fine and I returned to the nursery and the men to their places of rest. I laid there for some time waiting for another pain, but none came and the next thing I knew I was waking up in the morning ready for the day.

That day during the service, I shared with the church that the holy convocation would be of a prophetic nature. I had in mind to invite a prophet that I had known for years and I would contact him and a few other guests to come and join us at the convocation. I asked the church to be diligent to pray throughout the summer months in preparation for this time of separation and consecration unto the Lord.

I could sense, in the service, a growing excitement for the coming event and that the church was feeling good about what the Lord was directing us to do. I shared with them that the watchman needs to know what it is he is watching for and that the call to be sober minded concerning these things was important. I remembered reading something that really spoke to my heart during this time. "Discernment is not a matter of simply telling the difference between what is right and wrong; rather, it is the difference between right and almost right and the difference between truth and error is not a chasm, but a razor's edge."[1] The watchman must certainly be discerning and the call for discernment was now extremely important, considering the warning about compromise within the church.

Two days had passed since the event in the nursery. I was sitting home with my wife when I began to have chest pains. I told my wife that I wasn't feeling right. She asked me what I thought it was and I replied that I didn't know. She asked if I wanted to go to the hospital. She could see the concern on my face and she also knew about what had happened in the nursery. I said, "I'm having some chest pains." Several minutes had gone by and I said to my wife, "I think you had better take me to the hospital". All the way to the hospital the pains increased in severity and frequency. When we arrived at the emergency room I was in a great deal of pain. The doctors ordered the usual tests run, blood work, and an EKG to determine if it was heart related. They determined after several hours that it was not and sent us home with some Darvocet, a pain killer, and told me to call my primary care physician in the morning. During the night, my wife received an emergency call from a family member. She had to leave the house to tend to the emergency and when she arrived home she found me sleeping more comfortably than I had been before she left, so she decided not to disturb me and went downstairs to sleep on the couch. The next morning, I got up and went down stairs to see where my wife was. I stopped about halfway down the stairs seeing her laying on the couch and she awoke and asked me how I was. I told her that I felt much better, then returned to my bed.

My wife laid back on the couch and began to return to sleep, but was awakened by a phone call. It was a repair man whom we had contacted to come and look at our dishwasher which was not working properly. He was scheduled to come that morning and he was making sure someone would be home. After being awakened by the call, she laid back on the couch and once again was almost asleep when she was fully awakened by some strange noises from the bedroom upstairs. It was the first of many miracles that the repair man had called. If he had not called at just that time, my wife would never have heard what led her up the stairs. The following events my wife shared with me at the end of the ordeal because to this day, I have no recollection of them for the most part.

She ascended the stairs and as she entered the room she found me struggling to breath and my chest was heaving, which was the noise she had heard from downstairs. Once she got near enough to me, calling out my name several times, she realized that I was totally unresponsive to her call and her touch. Upon that realization, there was a panic that came over her. A thought went through her mind, "Lord should I try to save him? He always talks about being with you. Will he be angry with me if I don't let him go?" That thought very quickly faded and she reached for the phone to call 911. She called them and, as instructed, with the telephone between her head and her shoulder she began performing CPR. She continued until the ambulance arrived. She told the person on the phone that the downstairs door was locked and asked what she should do. The attendant told her to stop CPR, run downstairs as fast as she could and unlock the door for them. She did what she was told and they rushed up the stairs and into the bedroom to find me in cardiac arrest and not breathing. They quickly took me off the bed and put me on the backboard on the floor beside the bed, then began working on me, intubating me and doing compressions. They then used the defibrillator to restart my heart. She kept asking if they had a pulse and finally one of them said, "Yes, we have a faint pulse". They strapped me onto the board and carried me downstairs and out into the ambulance. She got into her car and followed us to the hospital.

At the hospital emergency room, they had to re-intubate me upon finding that the tube was not placed properly. They then had to stabilize me before transporting me to an affiliate hospital that had the latest technology for heart patients. During the time of stabilizing, contact was made with the doctors at the affiliate hospital to which I was being transferred. My wife was on the phone with them giving them the details of the event up to that point. They wanted assurance from my wife that I had not fallen and hit my head. They were concerned about possible brain injury in addition to the heart issue. Upon arriving at the hospital, it was determined that they would take me immediately to the catheterization lab to determine what was needed. It was the conclusion of the doctors treating me that I would need a coronary stent in one of my coronary arteries. There was a blockage and behind the blockage a blood clot had burst. They inserted the stent and placed me in the intensive care unit. Meanwhile, many from the church had gathered in the waiting room and began praying for me. They remembered the threat that I had received in the nursey and so they pleaded with the Lord to save me.

After the stent was placed in the artery the doctors determined that I should be placed in a drug induced coma so that they could begin therapeutic hypothermia, a fairly new technology developed to keep the brain from swelling during recovery. This therapy lowers the body's temperature to approximately ninety-three degrees. I remained in this state for three days. To make matters worse, it was determined that I had aspirated vomit during the cardiac event and had developed pneumonia. They began treating the pneumonia with antibiotics. Everyone knew at that point that there was a very low survival rate for those in my condition and all waited and prayed as the doctors did all they could to save my life. The enemy had already fulfilled his threat to kill me. Now, would the Lord sustain my life after I had been brought back?

The third day was used to slowly return my body temperature to normal. That evening, when it was clear that my body temperature had returned to normal, they began removing the equipment from my room that had been needed for the therapeutic hypothermia treatment. During that time, I unexpectedly awoke. My wife was by my side and saw that I had a fearful expression on my face and she knew that I had no recollection of what had happened, so she began to explain the events of the last three days. She explained why I had a feeding tube down my nose and tried to address all that she thought I needed to know to calm me.

Having been informed that I had regained consciousness, the cardiologists examined me and after much discussion decided to extubate me. My wife was in the room and they called for my adult children to be there for the extubation. Once the tube was removed it was apparent that I was still in somewhat of a confused state. All, but my wife, left the room and all were extremely encouraged that the tube had been removed and that I was conscious. They returned to the waiting room which for three days had become a prayer room and all rejoiced at the good news.

My wife shared with me all that had happened once again. In the middle of that conversation my wife heard a code blue sounding and the nurse who was just outside the door to my room and my wife looked down the hall to see for whom the alarm had sounded. When they turned their attention back to me, they saw that I had stopped breathing and realized that the alarm was for me. A group of nurses and doctors rushed into the room with the paddles and asked my wife to leave the room. She went out to the hallway and began sobbing. A woman who worked at the hospital assisting the patient's families came up to her and said, "look up not down" and she began to pray with her. The doctors came out of my room within a few minutes and said, "We've got him back". The medical staff were all bewildered and could not determine why it had happened. They immediately ordered blood work and awaited the labs. They placed me back into an unconscious state and reintubated me. Meanwhile, in the waiting room, more people had gathered and my wife went to them and said, "He flat lined again, but they got him back". They all immediately formed a circle, holding hands and began praying for a miracle. This back and forth struggle needed to be met with spiritual warfare.

At that point, the doctors did not believe it to be my heart that caused the cardiac arrest because they had already addressed the issue with my heart. After getting the lab results back, it was determined that I had low potassium. They started to administer potassium intravenously in hopes that it would correct the problem. However, the most challenging task for my nurse was finding the right combination of drugs that would keep me unconscious while my body was healing. She worked the whole day on her computer just outside my room and finally was satisfied that she had found the right combination. Her hard work paid off and I did remain in an unconscious state for the time needed. After a few days, they stopped administering the drugs and allowed me to regain consciousness.

It is a well-known fact that it is never a good thing to keep anyone intubated for an extended period, so the cardiologist and the pulmonologist met in my room to discuss trying to extubate me once again. Now that I was conscious, I desperately wanted the tube out and had be restrained to keep me from pulling it out. After a short discussion, as well as doing some cognitive tests on me, the consensus was that they would try once again to extubate me. My wife and family were present and it was carried out. Within a very short time I had trouble breathing normally and struggled to catch my breath. Sadly, it was necessary for me to be intubated for the fourth time.

Unfortunately, having been intubated four times, it was found that I had developed stridor which caused inflammation and swelling of the airways and vocal chords which follows prolonged intubation. For that reason, this condition is what prevented me from being able to breath unassisted. It was necessary to allow my vocal chords the time they needed to heal so that the swelling would abate before they tried to extubate me again. At that point, it was just a waiting game.

The pulmonologist later met with my wife privately to discuss what had happened. My wife knew that this was not a good situation. The length of time I had to be intubated posed its own set of problems. The longer a person does not breath on their own, the harder it is for the body to resume its natural function. My wife broke down and cried while talking with the doctor, expressing her concerns that I might have to live like that. The doctor agreed that it was one of her concerns as well, but said that all that can be done is to wait and pray for a quick healing of the vocal chords. My wife then went and informed the prayer team that remained in the waiting room and they once again began to pray for the specific need of the hour.

Within a few days, the consensus was that they would once again try to extubate me, but this time in an operating room atmosphere. The doctors felt that they would not only accomplish the extubation, but also assess any damage that had been done to the vocal chords. They discovered some scar tissue due to the many times I was intubated and extubated, but it appeared that the swelling had subsided and they felt confident that I could be successfully extubated. They went forward with the procedure and as a result I was able to breath on my own. My wife had been waiting for the procedure to finish and as they wheeled me by her, with no intubation tube, she thanked God and gave me a thumbs-up as I passed with a big smile on my face. There was, once again, much rejoicing in the waiting room when my wife shared with those gathered that it went well.

The nurses had been calling me the miracle man. They all agreed and stated as much, that it was a miracle that I survived. Added to the event itself was a vision I was given on the very first night in my room without the tube in. My son had brought me a CD player and a Christian CD to listen to. Evening had just entered the room and it was very dimly lit.

I had asked the nurse to turn on the CD player for me and she did and then left the room. I laid there listening to the music. It was an amazing song and as I listened to it, tears began to roll down my checks and I remember saying to the Lord, "Thank you so much for what you have done for me, Lord. Please show me why you have allowed me to live". As I spoke those words I began to see a vision. The television was off, but on the black screen I began to see, as if I were situated in amongst the stars, the edge of the universe. From out of this darkness far beyond me, like a giant waterfall, came thousands upon thousands of angels, pouring forth and heading towards me. As they drew closer I could see their beauty and their magnificence. They took no notice of me and began going right by me. Wanting to know where they were going, I turned and looked behind me and saw that the earth was their destination. They were dressed in green and gold transcendent robes. Coming from their being was a light that made their robes shine. I could see them yet could see through them at the same time. Every one of them had a sword drawn. They just kept coming from the edge of the universe. Just then the nurse came into the room and I asked her if she could see the angels. She quickly said no, there are no angels here and she became very alarmed and called for my wife to come to the room. My wife later told me that she was very concerned for me because I told her I was seeing angels. She told the nurse that she was exhausted and was going to go home and try and get a good night's sleep. The nurse told her she didn't think that it was a good idea and suggested that my wife might want to sleep in my room that night. I was unaware of what was going on until my wife informed me much later. She spent the night in the room and I insisted that they move my bed to be as close to her as possible, close enough to hold her hand. Of course, it went around the ICU that the miracle man had seen angels.

The next few days were very good for me and the doctors agreed that I could be moved out of the ICU. I was alert and able to communicate with the family and friends who came to visit and I could, for the first time, eat some soft foods by mouth. That evening I was wheeled to a kind of waiting room while a room was being prepared for me. As I sat in this waiting room I heard one of my doctors rebuking a nurse for calling me a miracle man. He was an atheist and asked her how she could believe in a loving God while seeing all the suffering that she has seen being an ICU nurse. I was trying to yell out my defense for the nurse, but my vocal chords had been so damaged that all I could do is whisper. Lest I forget, it is interesting that the very same doctor came into my room on the day that I was to be discharged and stood by the window as I sat in the chair by my bed. For a moment, he just stood there looking at me. Then he said, "When you walk out those doors, you better look up and give thanks, because you should not be alive". Then he wished me well and departed the room.

Eventually, I was moved out of the ICU and into a regular room. I remained there until I was able to walk without assistance. I could not believe how difficult it was for me to walk after having been bedbound for nineteen days. My wife brought me my Bible from home and a few books that I had been reading. I spent a great deal of time in prayer throughout the night, trying to determine the meaning of the whole thing. I was so thankful for the Lord's deliverance, for giving me my life back. However, I couldn't help but wonder why He had allowed it to happen. He had given me my life back for a purpose. That purpose, I reasoned, had to do with what we had been hearing from the Lord about the ancient paths and how, as we were discovering, the return to those ancient paths was to begin with a return to our Hebraic roots.

CHAPTER TWELVE

IN SEARCH
OF OUR HEBRAIC ROOTS

Through the search for the Hebraic roots of our faith, our church would begin a more intense study of the Old Testament scriptures than we had ever done before. Through the study it became apparent to us that biblical history was prophetic of future events, not only through the actual historical accounts, but from what was prophesied for the future as a reenactment of those events. Such is the case with the Exodus out of Egypt and the future exodus that will take place through the regathering of the exiles from all the nations of the world. It also became apparent to me that the role of Elijah in being sent by God to King Ahab was to address the "mixed worship" the people had been practicing. They were worshiping the God of Israel and the false god, Baal. When John the Baptist came preaching in the spirit and power of Elijah, he was addressing the same issue of "mixed worship". What was later to be called Rabbinic Judaism was the mixing of manmade traditions with the Torah of Moses. Jesus (Yeshua) was addressing this with the Pharisees throughout the New Testament almost every time we read of His encounters with them. Jesus taught the people to return to the only true Torah that was given to Moses on Mt. Sinai. This is biblical Judaism. The Christian church separated from the mixed worship that Israel had entered into, based upon the words of Jesus in the Gospels and the teachings of His disciples. Then the church did the same thing that Jesus addressed with Israel. The church began to add manmade traditions, many of them drawn out of the idolatry in the nations where they went to present the Gospel. I believe that the return to the Hebrew roots of the church, that is a move of the Holy Spirit over the course of the last several decades, is once again the same spirit and power of Elijah. I believe it is for the church and Judaism to turn from mixed worship and return to the Torah of the God of Israel. It is a call to turn back to the words given the fathers, to Abraham, Isaac, and Jacob and the Torah of Moses, to return to biblical Judaism. There are some who have accused us of trying to become Jews. You cannot become a Jew. You must be born a Jew. I do contend that those who follow Jesus will be returning to biblical Judaism. That is what He walked out during His life upon the earth. That is what He gave to Moses at Mt. Sinai. That is what He taught His disciples to bear witness to. If a Christian is a true follower of Jesus, then a Christian will walk as He did, in the truth that He lived.

The last six years since the heart attack have been the most amazing journey of my life. I knew that we were heading into something that would lead to strong reactions within the church. He has led us into a level of understanding His Word like we have never known before. For me, it has been as if I never really read the Bible before. Though I had read the Bible many times, it was never with the understanding that He has given to me since we, as a church, began this journey in search of the Hebraic roots of the Christian church. In this part of the book, I want to share with you the things that we have learned. I will only lightly touch upon each subject, because the well is so deep and I am still learning so much. I pray that the Lord will bless you with an understanding of these things, or at the very least, that He will create within you a hunger to seek out His truth and learn from Him.

"However, when He, the Spirit of truth, has come, He will guide you into all truth; for He will not speak on His own authority, but whatever He hears He will speak; and He will tell you things to come. He will glorify Me, for He will take of what is Mine and declare it to you" (John 16:13–14).

CHAPTER THIRTEEN

DESTINY SEEKERS

God communicates with us using words. When He gives a person or a church a vision, that vision is communicated through words and those words must carry a meaning that can be communicated to others. The words may come from the pages of scripture. They may come as that still small voice within us. They may be communicated in pictures, impressed either inwardly on the mind or outwardly in what we usually call a spiritual vision. The vision must then be actualized in real life. That means that those expectations expressed in the vision are to be actualized by deeds. In other words, the vision must be walked out.

For example, suppose I said to my ten-year-old son, "We're going swimming today". In speaking those words to him, in a sense, I have imparted a vision to him for going swimming along with the expectation that I can bring it about. We would not ordinarily speak of it in those terms. More than likely, we would say that I have given him the impression that I will take him swimming. However, many visions begin with an impression brought about by words. The scripture tells us that the "word of God is living and powerful" (Heb. 4:12). What that speaks to us is that when His word comes to us, it impresses upon us a course for life, either in the immediate or in regard to the future. Most often it entails both.

The development of a vision begins here, with that word of God, that impression that becomes a vision. After having imparted a vision to my son for going swimming, I then must actualize the expectation that I have given to him of going swimming. That means that I should develop the means to get there, in order to see the goal accomplished. That may be totally within my control to accomplish, or it may not. It may be a simple task for me to accomplish or it could be hampered by several things outside my control. I may not have a means of transportation and so I might have to acquire one. I may get interrupted by some life events that are out of my control and then must either work through them or determine to avoid being deterred by them to take my son swimming. Whatever the case may be, I have a responsibility to make the decisions that will either halt me or carry me forward.

Such is life when we are dealing on a purely earthly level within the natural realm or the natural scheme of things. It is up to us to acquire the assistance we need or to remove the obstacles in our way. However, when we are dealing with God, who is totally in control of everything and who's words can be counted on absolutely, then the words given from Him, resulting in a vision within us, are living and active. We are engaged with the One who is above the natural realm and who will actively participate in the actualization of the vision. We are in partnership (in covenant) with God, understanding that His will towards us is part of His covenant promise.

Though this vision comes from an unearthly realm and is governed by an unlimited being, the vision is still given to a being that dwells in the earth and who is, himself limited.

This earthly, limited being must then determine *to trust* in the heavenly, unlimited being to actualize the vision and aid in accomplishing the end goal. This is called "walking out the vision in faith". If we enter into a trusting relationship, exercising faith in the One who initiated the vision, then we have begun well. However, the environment in which we dwell, (the natural realm), will inevitably hinder and deter us if we allow it to. We must anticipate this and accept that this too is often a part of the divine intent and an integral part of the vision itself and not become discouraged. We are to "[. . .] count it all joy when you fall into various trials, knowing that the testing of your faith produces patience" (James 1:2–3).

In this covenant relationship with God, our faith will be tested in walking out His destiny for our lives. Though the vision may highlight the goal to be accomplished, like getting to the beach to go swimming, the journey there is to be discovered step-by-step and is also a part of the desired goal. We must seek God. He desires us to seek Him. This involves an active prayer life.

There is also an enemy who will try to lay hold of a vision that is given from God and that enemy will do all that he can to deter us from fulfilling our destiny and God's vision for us. His greatest weapons are fear of man, fear of failure, and an appeal to the selfishness resident within the Adamic nature: the lust of the flesh, the lust of the eyes, and the boastful pride of life. However, once again, because of the divine hand engaged in the outworking of this vision, even our enemies' efforts are used by God for the advancement of the vision if we love Him and walk in faith. "And we know that all things work together for good to those who love God, to those who are the called according to His purpose" (Rom. 8:28). He who would receive and embrace a vision must look above to where the author of the vision dwells, in order to gain the clarity and strength which comes through faith in Him. When I say that the Lord has birthed within me a vision, I then have a responsibility to continue to look above to the One who gave it, so that He can begin to define the vision in such a way that it becomes actualized. Otherwise, it remains an empty vision.

The vision that the Lord gave to me for the church that I pastor began with these words, "I want you to become destiny seekers". The vision was apparently for the whole church, but there is a call for each individual within the church to become a destiny seeker. The unfolding of the meaning of that phrase will be the what, how, why, and when of it. What is a destiny seeker? How do we become destiny seekers? Why are we called to such a vision? When do we begin to actualize the living of it?

As I looked to the Lord to unfold the answers to these questions, I had to realize that it is not just the answer to the questions, but the obedience to embrace the answers and walk it out. The answer to the first question, what is a destiny seeker, came as an unfolding answer. As we moved from one place to another within the vision, we picked up things along the way that further defined and directed us.

Every Christian should be a destiny seeker, which is really just one attribute of a disciple. However, because words carry special meanings for people, the Lord often uses words in such a way to give them a distinctiveness that will initiate a path for people to walk on. The attribute or distinctive meaning of "destiny seeker" comes from Colossians 3:1–3.

"If then you were raised with Christ, seek those things which are above, where Christ is, seated at the right hand of God.

Set your mind on things above, not on things on the earth.
For you died, and your life [Zōē] is hidden with Christ in
God" (Col. 3:1–3).

The Greek word rendered (life) in this passage is Zōē. The definition of Zōē is used in the New Testament, "of life as a principle, life in the absolute sense, life as God has it, '[. . .] that which the Father has in Himself, and which He gave to the Incarnate Son to have in Himself [. . .]' [John 5:26] and 'which the Son manifested in the world' [1 John 1:2]. 'From this life man has become alienated in consequence of the Fall, [Eph. 4:18] and of this life men become partakers through faith in the Lord Jesus Christ, [John 3:15], who becomes its Author to all such as trust in Him, [Acts 3:15], and who is therefore said to be 'the life' of the believer, [Col. 3:4], for the life that He gives He maintains, [John 6:35,63]. This life is not merely a principle of power and mobility, however, for it has moral associations which are inseparable from it, as of holiness and righteousness.'" [1]

A path is the means, the direction, the channel, the way, and the course to a destination. It can be defined as "a course of conduct" and "the path of virtue". [2] According to Colossians 3:3, "our life is hidden in Christ", then only Christ can reveal that life or that destiny, that is our life in Him (Gal. 2:20).

Collins English Dictionary contains a definition of "destiny" that is well suited to the Christian, "the inner purpose of a life that can be discovered and realized". [3] I believe that one of the reasons that Christ gives us a vision is so that we can discover and realize the inner purpose of a life in Him, whether it be as an individual or for the church. The way in which this inner purpose of life is discovered for a Christian is by looking to Christ where it is hidden. That life is our destiny in Him. "[. . .] Seek those things which are above, where Christ is [. . .] Set your mind on things above, not on things on the earth" (Col. 3:1–2). There is no other way.

Destiny seekers is not a program within the church; it is a way of life for those within the church who choose to make the commitment. Not all who are a part of the church will want to make the required commitment to become a destiny seeker; but for those who do, it will require taking hold of the vision and actively participating in it. If the vision is for the church and if the greatest attribute of the church is love, then we have the necessary virtue to move forward with this vision.

Those who want to become Destiny Seekers must make a whole commitment and covenant together with others who will make the same commitment. Covenant implies accountability and the accountability that we must have is rooted in living for a cause greater than ourselves, the cause of Christ. The Lord desires to teach us, just as we desire to teach our children how to acquire the best things in life. What is the greatest thing that we can teach to our young people and our children? To seek after their destiny in God and within the kingdom of God. What is the framework of those who would become destiny seekers? I would suggest the following destiny seekers commitment:

DESTINY SEEKERS COMMITMENT
Declare Your Citizenship – Eph. 2:19, Phil. 3:17–4:1
Stand with Israel – Gen. 12:3, Isa. 62:1
Seek the Things Above – Col. 3:1–2, Heb. 3:1

Be Watchful – Amos 3:7, Matt. 24:32–35
Alert and Discerning – 2 Tim. 3:1–7, Eph. 5:15–21
Know the Word of God – Heb. 4:12, Isa. 5:13, Hos. 4:6
Walk in the Spirit – Rom. 8:5–8, John 16:13
Pray and Meditate – Phil. 4:6–8, 1 Thess. 5:16–18

DECLARE YOUR CITIZENSHIP – EPH. 2:19, PHIL. 3:17–4:1

An individual is considered a good citizen if he/she honors the laws of the land, supports the proclamations of the government and renders unto Caesar that which is Caesars. The same is true of the kingdom of God. We declare our citizenship not only by our confession, but also by honoring God and rendering unto God that which is God's (Matt. 22:21). This literally means giving Him first place in our lives by honoring the Lord's day as holy and giving Him the first fruits of all our labors. If these, which are the two most valuable assets in life (time and possessions), are given to honor Him then the lesser things will surely be in line with His will and purpose for our lives. Therefore, a destiny seeker must first be true to the word of God, the proclamations of the King who rules and reigns in the kingdom of God. This is where the path begins for all who would travel it, fulfill this vision and in doing so you glorify the Lord.

PRACTICAL APPLICATION

The practical application of this step is entirely up to the individual to maintain. In doing so, the individual will reap the blessings of the Lord associated with obedience to His will. The salvation aspect of the covenant of God is unconditional in that its fulfillment depends entirely on God and solely on faith in His word. The covenant blessings are conditional, based on our obedience to the covenant. God is not mocked, whatsoever a man sows that shall he also reap. I would add that sharing the gospel with people on a regular basis is certainly a part of declaring your citizenship. This means staying alert to the opportunities that He gives to us, looking for those divine appointments.

STAND WITH ISRAEL – GEN. 12:3, ISA. 62:1

"I will bless those who bless you, and I will curse him who curses you; and in you all the families of the earth shall be blessed" (Gen. 12:3).

"For Zion's sake I will not hold My peace, and for Jerusalem's sake I will not rest, until her righteousness goes forth as brightness, and her salvation as a lamp that burns" (Isa. 62:1).

We should stand with Israel because they are the people of God. "Remember His covenant forever, the word which He commanded, for a thousand generations, the covenant which He made with Abraham, and His oath to Isaac, and confirmed it to Jacob for a statute, to Israel *for* an everlasting covenant [. . .]" (1 Chron. 16:15–17). God says to Abraham, "In your seed all the nations of the earth shall be blessed [. . .]" (Gen. 22:18).

"I will bless those who bless you, and I will curse him who curses you; and in you all the families of the earth shall be blessed" (Gen. 12:3).

PRACTICAL APPLICATION

Pray for Israel on a daily basis. Pray for peace within her borders, for the Christians who live there, for God's will to be done in and through her, for her protection through divine intervention according to the word of God. Pray for the day to come soon when Israel will say, "'Blessed is He who comes in the name of the Lord [. . .]'" (Matt. 23:39) in acknowledgement of Jesus Christ as Messiah. Know the Jewish history and the promises God has made to them. Understand how God has kept and is still keeping His word so that you can communicate these promises to those who would persecute the Jews.

Become a member of associations or para-church groups which actively support Israel, such as Joel Rosenberg's ministry, The Joshua Fund, Christians United for Israel, Ezra International, and others. These organizations support Israel and are very fertile soil in which to sow your talents and your finances.

SEEK THE THINGS ABOVE – COL. 3:1–2, HEB. 3:1

"If then you were raised with Christ, seek those things which are above, where Christ is, sitting at the right hand of God. Set your mind on things above, not on things on the earth" (Col. 3:1–2).

"Therefore, holy brethren, partakers of the heavenly calling, consider the Apostle and High Priest of our confession, Christ Jesus [. . .]" (Heb. 3:1).

PRACTICAL APPLICATION

Get involved with a prayer ministry. Fast at least once a week, spending time in personal devotions. Keep a journal of your conversations with the Lord. Choose wisely what activities you give yourself to and serve in the church wherever and whenever you can. Some examples include getting involved in intercessory prayer groups, youth activities, children's church, and supporting home group meetings or mid-week services by being present. All of these are ways to help build up the kingdom of God and to avoid too much time given to the kingdoms of this world.

BE WATCHFUL – AMOS 3:7, MATT. 24:32–35

"Surely the Lord GOD does nothing, unless He reveals His secret to His servants the prophets" (Amos 3:7).

"Now learn this parable from the fig tree: When its branch has already become tender and puts forth leaves, you know that summer is near. So, you also, when you see all these things, know that it is near—at the doors? Assuredly, I say to you, this generation will by no means pass away till all these things take place. Heaven and earth will pass away, but My words will by no means pass away" (Matt. 24: 32–35).

PRACTICAL APPLICATION

Help to develop the vision, destiny seekers, by drawing near to God and praying for His direction for walking out the vision. This is a vision for the church as well as a vision for our lives as individuals within the church. It is therefore important that we share what we feel the Lord is speaking to us or encouraging us to do as a part of the whole. Prepare your household for the coming days and what they may bring. Don't be caught unaware or unprepared. We are called to be ready for His appearing and are to be found doing the work of the kingdom when He comes.

ALERT AND DISCERNING – 2 TIM. 3:1–7, EPH. 5:15–21

"But know this, that in the last days perilous times will come: For men will be lovers of themselves, lovers of money, boasters, proud, blasphemers, disobedient to parents, unthankful, unholy, unloving, unforgiving, slanderers, without self-control, brutal, despisers of good, traitors, headstrong, haughty, lovers of pleasure rather than lovers of God, having a form of godliness but denying its power. And from such people turn away! For of this sort are those who creep into households and make captives of gullible women loaded down with sins, led away by various lusts, always learning and never able to come to the knowledge of the truth" (2 Tim. 3:1–7).

"See then that you walk circumspectly, not as fools but as wise, redeeming the time, because the days are evil. Therefore, do not be unwise, but understand what the will of the Lord is. And do not be drunk with wine, in which is dissipation; but be filled with the Spirit, speaking to one another in psalms and hymns and spiritual songs, singing and making melody in your heart to the Lord, giving thanks always for all things to God the Father in the name of our Lord Jesus Christ, submitting to one another in the fear of God" (Eph. 5: 15–21).

PRACTICAL APPLICATION

Ephesians tells us to redeem the time. That means that we need to be giving ourselves to those things that have eternal value first and foremost and the things that have temporal value must be of secondary importance. We are to understand what the will of the Lord is, which we are assured we can know if we will ask, seek, and knock (Matt. 7:7–8).

KNOW THE WORD OF GOD – HEB. 4:12, ISA. 5:13, HOS. 4:6

"For the word of God is living and powerful, and sharper than any two-edged sword, piercing even to the division of soul and spirit, and of joints and marrow, and is a discerner of the thoughts and intents of the heart" (Heb. 4:12).

"Therefore My people have gone into captivity, because they have no knowledge [. . .]*"* (Isa. 5:13).

"My people are destroyed for lack of knowledge [. . .]*"* (Hos. 4:6).

PRACTICAL APPLICATION

Take notes during teachings and study what is being taught. Learn to memorize scripture by grouping passages according to subject. The more the Word is in you, the more the Holy Spirit can use the Word to guide you during times of prayer, so that you are praying the very Word of God. He can also use the Word within you to more effectively witness to others or to confirm what is of God and to discern what is not of God. Get into holy conversations with brethren about the Word of God. The more you discuss the Word, the more the Word becomes a part of you. Attend men or women's meetings where you can learn how to accurately handle the Word of God. It is written, "Be diligent to present yourself approved to God, a worker who does not need to be ashamed, rightly dividing the word of truth" (2 Tim. 2:15).

WALK IN THE SPIRIT – ROM. 8:5–8, JOHN 16:13

"For those who live according to the flesh set their minds on the things of the flesh, but those who live according to the Spirit, the things of the Spirit. For to be carnally minded is death, but to be spiritually minded is life and peace. Because the carnal mind is enmity against God; for it is not subject to the law of God, nor indeed can be. So then, those who are in the flesh cannot please God" (Rom. 8:5–8).

"However, when He, the Spirit of truth, has come, He will guide you into all truth; for He will not speak on His own authority, but whatever He hears He will speak; and He will tell you things to come" (John 16:13).

PRACTICAL APPLICATION

Develop the habit of asking the Holy Spirit to guide you by setting your mind on the things of the Spirit. Many Christians only think about what the Lord desires for them to do or say once a day during devotions, some not even that often. If we truly desire to walk by the Spirit, with the Spirit and in the Spirit, we need to decide to talk with the Spirit throughout the day. Little reminders can help us form such a habit. For some people, it is wearing a cross or a pin on their clothing somewhat like the Jews who wear a tallit. For some it is a printed scripture stuck to the dashboard of their car or keeping the car radio on a Christian station. Do whatever you can think of that works to remind you. It is essential that destiny seekers are mindful that they are the Lord's and that He has given them the Holy Spirit to direct and empower them. You can also get in the habit of asking those who are walking out this vision with you what they have heard from the Lord each time you see them and invite them to do the same with you, thus initiating a holy conversation.

PRAY AND MEDITATE – PHIL. 4:6–8, 1 THESS. 5:16–18

"Be anxious for nothing, but in everything by prayer and supplication, with thanksgiving, let your requests be made known to God; and the peace of God, which surpasses all understanding, will guard your hearts and minds through Christ Jesus. Finally, brethren, whatever things are true, whatever things are noble, whatever things are just, whatever things are pure, whatever things are lovely, whatever things are of good report, if there is any virtue and if there is anything praiseworthy—meditate on these things" (Phil. 4:6–8).

"Rejoice always, pray without ceasing, in everything give thanks; for this is the will of God in Christ Jesus for you" (1 Thess. 5:16–18).

PRACTICAL APPLICATION

Learn how to pray by praying with those who are prayer warriors. Learn how to meditate on the Scriptures and allow them to develop in your mind. This is often the way that the Holy Spirit will bring you into new revelation.

THE CALLING

We are not called to be ordinary, but extraordinary
We are not called to the usual, but to the unusual
We are not called to the rehearsed, but to the spontaneous
We are not called to the expected, but to the unexpected
We Are Called to Be Ready for His Appearing

"I can do all things through Christ who strengthens me" (Phil. 4:13). This verse tells us that if we have the faith of a mustard seed, we can do whatever God is calling upon us to do. Fear and doubt are the enemies of faith. When we look at what challenges us and simply say, "Oh, I don't think I can do that, I don't have the money to go there, I don't have the time, I'm not very good at that, or my spouse would be upset if I left him/her alone" or whatever the excuse is, then we have set faith aside and opted for fear and doubt. Does God call us to difficult things? Yes. That is how He develops faith in us. Does God call us to where He cannot take us or provide for us or intervene for us? No; Absolutely not! This undertaking requires faith and must be a statement of faith if it is to mean anything at all.

WE ARE NOT CALLED TO THE USUAL, BUT TO THE UNUSUAL

"Beloved, do not think it strange concerning the fiery trial which is to try you, as though some strange thing happened to you [. . .]" (1 Peter 4:12). We don't need to be discipled in the usual, everyday circumstances of life once we have learned the elementary principles of the kingdom of God. We do, however, need to be guided and directed through those unusual circumstances, those fiery trials and ordeals which equip the saints of God for the work of service that glorifies our Lord and Savior. If you commit to being a destiny seeker, you can expect that the Holy Spirit will lead you into a destiny that is full of challenges that are meant to conform you to the image of Christ, because that is the ultimate destiny of every born-again believer. We must train our minds to think God's thoughts. His thoughts are contained in His Word and are also brought to us by the Holy Spirit. Thoughts such as these:

My brethren, count it all joy when you fall into various trials, knowing that the testing of your faith produces patience. But let patience have its perfect work, that you may be perfect and complete, lacking nothing (James 1:2–4).

It takes training to think God's thoughts after him, but that is a part of our destiny.

WE ARE NOT CALLED TO THE REHEARSED, BUT TO THE SPONTANEOUS

"The wind blows where it wishes, and you hear the sound of it, but cannot tell where it comes from and where it goes. So is everyone who is born of the Spirit" (John 3:8). Jesus said, "Most assuredly, I say to you, the Son can do nothing of Himself, but what He sees the Father do; for whatever He does, the Son also does in like manner" (John 5:19).

Jesus didn't always know what was coming next. He spent time with the Father in prayer and the Father showed Him what He was to do. The Father assured Jesus, by the Holy Spirit, that He would always lead Him, give Him what He was to speak, and show Him what He was to do. None of it was rehearsed. Jesus had to be spontaneous and so did His disciples. Many Christians don't witness because they are fearful that they won't know what to say if they are put on the spot. Jesus told His disciples, "[. . .] do not worry about how or what you should answer, or what you should say. For the Holy Spirit will teach you in that very hour what you ought to say" (Luke 12:11–12). Once again, the practical outworking of this call to be ready is a matter of faith and trust in the Lord.

WE ARE NOT CALLED TO THE EXPECTED, BUT TO THE UNEXPECTED

2 Timothy 4:2 says, "Preach the word! Be ready in season and out of season." Be ready! One cannot be ready unless he has done his part to prepare. Then having done his part, he can trust the Lord to accomplish His will in and through him. Doing our part consists of all of the above, so that when the unexpected arises, and it will, we will not panic. Instead, with sound judgment, we will rise above the circumstances and face the unexpected with confidence in Christ.

WE ARE CALLED TO BE READY FOR HIS APPEARING

"Therefore you also be ready, for the Son of Man is coming at an hour you do not expect" (Matt. 24:44).

CHAPTER FOURTEEN

THE CONVOCATION

I had the heart attack on August 11, 2010. I was in the hospital for twenty-one days and returned home on Wednesday, September first. The hospital arranged for a news crew to come to the house a few weeks later to interview me and to film the interview since I was, as they put it, an amazing success story for the hospital. They wanted to use the story on media for fund raising. Even though this was exciting, I wanted to get back to the church and resume planning for the upcoming convocation. It was scheduled for the second weekend in October.

The church was a small church, with about forty-five adults at that time, and almost as many children. We had already rented a place for the Convocation.; the setting was beautiful. It had a campsite feel to it, set in the woods with a large pond, many cabins, and a main lodge where we would hold our gatherings. It was the fall and the leaves that were left on the trees, at that time, were beautifully colored, red, orange, and yellow.

One of the wonderful things about living in New Hampshire is that you get to see the splendor of His creation change from the beautiful deep green of summer to the bursting forth of color in the fall. I live on a mountain and driving to the church every day, in the fall, I would find myself thanking the Lord of creation for the beauty of His creation. As I descend the mountain road from my house, I can see the many other mountains off in the distance, full of color and the great Lake Winnipesauke reflecting those colors on its waters. I can also see Mt. Washington off in the distance, standing taller than the other mountains as if to suggest some sort of royalty. Adding to its majestic look, this mountain is also the first to be crowned with snow as winter approaches.

The convocation was a mixture of excitement and disappointment. Many of the people received personal prophecies from the prophet that I had invited to attend and yet there was a constant interruption in the times of worship, which became the subject of conversation in the dining hall. The convocation was only a weekend long, so we felt it was important to regain our focus as quickly as possible. We determined to focus on prayer and several of the cabins hosted small intimate times of prayer. I believe that it was in these gatherings that we received the most precious things from the Lord. I wouldn't say that the convocation was a catastrophe or a great success, but I do believe that the most important thing to come out of it was a certain sense that the direction of the church was changing drastically. The holy conversation that we had engaged in, and continued to remind one another of, had given the whole church a sense of purpose. We sensed the Lord interacting with His people within these conversations. The confirmation that would be brought to individuals as they conversed with others continued to give us the sense that the Holy Spirit was birthing something.

We would often return to the prophetic word that I had received during the time of prayer with the men just before my heart attack. We were studying His Word to find some sort of compass, some sort of solid direction for going forward. It was during this time that we discovered Jeremiah 6:16, "Thus says the LORD: 'Stand in the ways and see, and ask for the old paths, where the good way is, and walk in it; then you will find rest for your souls [. . .]" That verse captured me and began to work in me. I studied these ancient paths with a hunger that would not be quenched until I found where they began, where they led, and how we could begin to walk in them. The Spirit of the Lord seemed to be leading me to things I had never seen before in the Scriptures. These things were disturbing to me and to the men and women within the church that I would share them with. These were things that seemed so contrary to what we had been taught and held to throughout our Christian lives. I prayed that the Lord would show me how to share these things in such a way that would not frighten the people. I knew that these things would disturb the people as they were disturbing me, but were they meant to disturb us, to awaken us? To be honest, I was both excited and frightened.

We held men's meetings every Tuesday evening and I decided to first begin sharing these things for discussion at these meetings. I was looking for confirmation wherever I could find it and I began to search online, using various scriptures, beginning with the phrase, "the ancient paths". As soon as I put the phrase into the search engine a flood of sites came up. I couldn't believe what I was finding. The Lord had been speaking to thousands all over the country, indeed all over the world, concerning these ancient paths. What I thought was so unique to us, I found, was not at all unique. As a matter of fact, it seemed that it was almost old news.

I know that there is a great deal of controversy over what is being called a return to the Hebraic roots of Christianity. Some call it the Hebraic Roots Movement and much of traditional Christianity is suspicious of it or outright opposed to it. My desire was not, and is not, to join some movement, rather to find the truth of God's word wherever I could. Among those who were seeking to return to the Hebraic roots of their faith, I found a great deal of truth. I found that the most trusted of those who were teaching the Hebraic perspective of Scripture, were those who were not promoting a cause. These trusted destiny seekers were not more interested in proving someone wrong than simply finding the truth and sharing it with humility and love.

I realized at some point that our church had begun to walk on these ancient paths. We had, as a community of believes in Jesus Christ, turned our attention back to seeking His way and not just *a way* of walking in His word. Still, looking for confirmation as we struggled to let go of things that we had held to for generations within our Christian families, the Lord blessed me with another dream. Directly after the dream ended I awoke knowing that the Lord was speaking something through the dream and that I should get up and write it down, but I was tired. It was 3:00 a.m. and I hadn't really slept well up to that point, and so rather than getting up, I began going through the dream in my mind and repeating a particular Hebrew word, which was significant to the dream. It was my hope that I would not forget it come morning. I knew that I was somewhat familiar with the word, but could not remember its meaning at the time. When I was convinced that I had rehearsed the dream and the word enough I allowed myself to return to sleep.

When I arose that morning, I could remember only bits and pieces of the dream, but not all the details. I could not remember the Hebrew word that I had heard, only that it was a Hebrew word. I was upset with myself knowing that I should have gotten up and recorded the dream and the Hebrew word when I awoke from the dream. Later that morning I tried sharing the dream with my wife hoping to remember more of the details and especially the Hebrew word. As I said, I remembered recognizing the word in my dream, but I could not remember what the word was.

That afternoon I spent some time in prayer and confessed to the Lord my disobedience of having not gotten up to write down the dream. I asked the Lord to forgive me and to bring the dream back to me. After a time of prayer, I was tired from not having slept well so I decided to lay down for what I call my old man nap. As soon as I had laid down on the couch I began asking the Lord to give me the dream again, should I fall asleep, but my request had no sooner left my mind, when the dream in all of its details and the Hebrew word came rushing back into my mind. I saw the dream, this time in a waking vision and the Hebrew word "She'alti'el".

I quickly got up from the couch and went to search for the word and its meaning and found it within minutes. It was indeed a Hebrew word and its meaning is "I have asked of God". [1] The root of the word is 'sha'al' which means 'to ask, inquire, beg'. It is used repeatedly in the Old Testament of men and women asking God for guidance. In both 1 and 2 Samuel, it is used to describe David, inquiring of the Lord. It is also used in contrast with the leaders of Israel who, asked not counsel at the mouth of the Lord. In Isaiah 30:1–2 it is also present, "'Woe to the rebellious children,' says the LORD, who take counsel, but not of Me". I believed that what the Lord was telling me was that because I had asked to be led by Him into His truth, he had given me the truth that I am about to share with you. The Lord, in His faithfulness, not only brought back the dream, but He also gave me the interpretation of the dream.

THE DREAM

In the dream, I was kneeling and was praying before what appeared to be a large stone altar. As I was praying I was interrupted by a stirring to the left of me and out from a dimly lit area came two hands bearing a large clay pot and the pot was offered to me. I could not see beyond the hands that held the pot, or who was extending it to me, because they remained in the dimly lit area of the room. I took the pot from their hands and went back over to the front of the altar where it was much lighter because the sun was coming in from a window just above the altar. Positioned there, I could look and see the contents of the pot. As I looked down into the pot it was apparent that it was full of honey. It was a very clear yellow kind of thick substance and I could smell its sweet fragrance. I somehow knew what I was to do with the honey. I stepped up to the altar where I could see, for the first time, the top of the altar and noticed that running across the top of the altar towards the front, was a kind of canal or channel carved into the stone surface. It ran across from left to right and remained open at the right side of the altar. I knew that I was to pour the honey into this canal. As I was doing so, I heard the word "She'alti'el" spoken loudly. The honey began to run form where I had poured it and off the altar at the opening on the right side. Then I looked down to see where the honey was going and as I looked, the floor to the right of the altar was opened up and there were many people gathered some distance below the altar. The honey was dripping from the altar and the people had their hands lifted up and were allowing the honey to flow into their hands. Their heads were lifted up toward the altar and there was such joy on their faces. That is where the dream ended.

THE INTERPRETATION OF THE DREAM

In the dream, I had been kneeling before an altar, which speaks of sacrifice and it is only by the sacrifice of Christ that we have access to the Father. The altar clearly represents the sacrifice of Christ through which we can approach the Father.

"For men indeed swear by the greater, and an oath for confirmation is for them an end of all dispute. Thus God, determining to show more abundantly to the heirs of promise the immutability of His counsel, confirmed it by an oath, that by two immutable things, in which it is impossible for God to lie, we might have strong consolation, who have fled for refuge to lay hold of the hope set before us. This hope we have as an anchor of the soul, both sure and steadfast, and which enters the Presence behind the veil, where the forerunner has entered for us, even Jesus, having become High Priest forever according to the order of Melchizedek" (Heb. 6:16–20).

"Therefore, brethren, having boldness to enter the Holiest by the blood of Jesus, by a new and living way which He consecrated for us, through the veil, that is, His flesh, and having a High Priest over the house of God, let us draw

near with a true heart in full assurance of faith [. . .]"
(Heb. 10:19–22).

"For through Him we both have access by one Spirit to the Father" (Eph. 2:18).

The altar is also the place of intercession. The word "She'alti'el", meaning "I have asked of God" [2] was an acknowledgement that because I had been praying and asking of God, that I was heard and an answer was to be given. The answer was to come from the hand of God and the honey represented the Word of God.

A study on the word "honey" produced the following information. The first stage of education for a Jew was called Bet Seffer, the name means "house of the book."[3] I remembered listening to a teaching where the teacher shared that there was a saying in Judaism about the importance to the Jewish people of educating their children. "Under the age of six, we do not receive a child as a pupil, but from six upwards, accept him and stuff him with Torah like an ox." [4]

There was a tradition among Rabbis who taught Torah. They would often begin by introducing the Word of God to the children, through pouring honey into the hands of the students. The children, at six years of age, would get very excited because honey was a very special treat. So, the children would have this honey in their hands, they would smell its sweetness, and then the Rabbi would tell the students to taste the honey, which was a very precious commodity in those days. As these children were licking this honey off their fingers and tasting its sweetness, the Rabbi would then tell them that the Torah, the written Word of God that they were about to begin to study, was like the honey and that they should know of its sweetness, its taste, and how good it is. They did this so that, from the beginning, the children would desire the Word of God as something that was precious and sweet and they would associate it with this honey.

Scripture tells us that honey was not only known for its sweetness but also for its medicinal qualities. Proverbs 16:24 demonstrates this, "Pleasant words are like a honeycomb, sweetness to the soul and health to the bones." God's words are pleasant. His words bring healing to us, they sweeten our lives, and comfort us when we are in distress. His word can restore hope and remove the bitterness from our lives, "[. . .] sweetness to the soul and health to the bones."

Honey also indicated or symbolized abundance and prosperity. In Deuteronomy 32:13, speaking of Israel, the Almighty speaks through His prophet, Moses and declares, "He made him ride in the heights of the earth, that he might eat the produce of the fields; He made him draw honey from the rock, and oil from the flinty rock [. . .]" In at least twenty instances, the Old Testament calls the promised land a "land flowing with milk and honey."

In my dream, honey was the Word of God flowing unto the people of God who were standing and waiting and calling upon the Lord. The fact that the floor was opened up indicated that there was no partition, no barrier between the people of faith and the throne of grace. Those who acknowledged the sacrifice of Jesus Christ on the altar of God have those blessings that flow from heaven.

What I sensed that the Lord was saying in this dream is that if we seek Him, if we ask in faith believing, if we will give ourselves to intercession or She'alti'el, then the Word of the Lord will flow to us like honey, it will be sweetness to the soul and health to the bones. It will be that valued gift from our heavenly Father to sustain us in these last days and to instruct us in His way. The Word of God would pour down upon them in the days ahead through the revelation given by His Holy Spirit. I saw three important elements in the dream. The first was intercession or She'alti'el, "I have asked of God". The second was recognition, which is to acknowledge what God is doing in this hour. He told us at the beginning of that year that He would speak to His people in dreams and visions and that His people were to acquire knowledge, specifically a knowledge concerning the days in which we live. We were to seek a prophetic unveiling of end time prophecies. The third important element was position; we were to position ourselves before God with our hands lifted up in expectation of His Word pouring forth and taste and see that the Lord is good.

One week later, as I was standing in a church service, one of the parishioners came over to me and said, "There is a prophetic conference in Florida in a few weeks and I believe the Lord wants you to attend." I said, "I will certainly pray about it." He replied, "I'll send you some information on it." I thought about it on the way home that day. I had not been to a conference for many years. What would my wife think about me going off so soon after my heart attack? There were only a few weeks to decide.

He did get the information to me and said that he knew of a place we could stay. It was with his sister's family who lived in Florida very close to where the conference was to be held and he was willing to attend the conference with me. A short time later we decided to go. I talked with my brother and he seemed interested in going. He said he would think about it and within a few days had made the decision to go. It seemed everything was indicating we should attend the conference, including my wife who felt better knowing that I would be traveling with my older brother and would be with someone familiar with the area as well.

One of the speakers at the conference was Dr. Richard Booker. I had never heard this brother speak and did not know of his writings. He began to speak about things that I had never heard before, things like celebrating Jesus in the Biblical Feasts. Almost immediately, as he began to speak, the Lord brought to my mind the dream about the altar and the honey. I knew that I was to take back to the church what Dr. Booker was sharing and pour it over them like honey. After Dr. Booker finished speaking there was a break before the next speaker so I went over to talk with him and to share with him and his wife the dream that I had been given. I shared with him that I believed that what he had taught was that honey. He hugged me and blessed me. I returned home with a few of his books, which the Lord used to lead us further on in our walk upon the ancient paths.

Several people who have visited our little church from other states during the summer months have asked how a whole congregation was turned from traditional Christianity to pursue their Hebraic roots. They have all stated that it doesn't usually happen that way. It is usually a few individuals within the traditional church who are moved by the Holy Spirit to begin seeking their Hebraic roots and are forced to leave their church in search of others who are hearing the same thing. That is one of the reasons I share this testimony. The only answer I can give is that the Great Conductor orchestrated the whole thing. There were a few couples who left. They could not abandon the traditions that they had grown up in but, for the most part, the Lord was faithful to give most parishioners an ear to hear and a desire for the ancient paths.

The rest of the chapters in this book will be a brief study in what we have learned traveling these ancient paths. Again, I pray that the Lord will use these words to excite you to pursue the truth of God in a day when His truth is truly sanctifying His people and separating out a remnant for His glory.

"I do not pray that You should take them out of the world, but that You should keep them from the evil one. They are not of the world, just as I am not of the world. Sanctify them by Your truth. Your word is truth" (John 17:15–17).

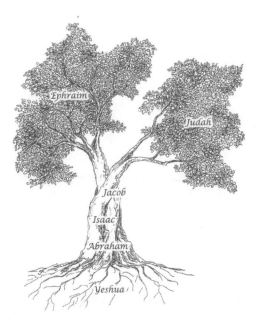

CHAPTER FIFTEEN

THE HEBRAIC
ROOTS OF OUR FAITH

Where does one begin to look for the roots of our faith and why should we care to look for the roots of our faith? I would say that it is important that we be stirred to consider the roots of our faith to know that what we believe is founded upon the Word of God and only the Word of God. I further believe that a faith in God must be an intelligent faith and not just some mystical belief in a God that has no true history or no solid pronouncements declaring who He is and how we are to relate to Him. Therefore, I believe that the roots of our faith must be found in the Word of God and not in the traditions of men. Religion is not necessarily truth. There are many religions in the world, and they are full of contrasting views of who God is and how we are to serve His purposes in the earth. Even in the culture we live in today, there is a quest by many to research their heritage, desiring to link the past with the present. Isn't that what we do as Christians when we determine to search for our Hebrew roots? Are we not attempting to link the past with the present to understand the stream that will lead to the future?

OUR HERITAGE – OUR INHERITANCE

Today, many individuals in the secular world desire to know their ancestry and family history. They devote time to researching records of past generations to understand their "roots" and to find out what uniquely distinguishes them and all those tied to a family name. Knowing one's heritage produces a greater understanding of and respect for owning one's inheritance. This search parallels what is taking place today in the spiritual realm. The Holy Spirit is leading many within Christianity to desire, discover and embrace the roots of the foundation of their faith in Jesus Christ, which make them members of the Hebrew family of God, chosen, distinguished, and unique. As believers in Christ, our inheritance is preserved in biblical Judaism, also referred to as the Old Testament.

How does one understand what this means? It requires allowing the Holy Spirit to guide us as we devote time to studying the whole Word of God, both the written Word (Old and New Testaments), and the Living Word (Jesus/ Yeshua). Then, we can apprehend what it means to belong to a people called by His almighty name and a return to our true foundation.

WHAT ARE THE HEBRAIC ROOTS OF OUR FAITH?

No one within traditional Christianity would deny that what is called the church today had its beginning within Judaism. The Messiah Himself was a Jew, of Jewish parents, of the tribe of Judah, a descendant of King David. The Genealogy of Jesus Christ is recorded for us in Matthew 1:1–17, "The book of the genealogy of Jesus Christ, the Son of David, the Son of Abraham [. . .] And Jacob begot Joseph the husband of Mary, of whom was born Jesus who is called Christ." Therefore, when we are looking to trace our roots, we find that we are drawn back to Jesus, our Messiah, who is called the "Head of the body, the church".

"And He is the head of the body, the church, who is the beginning, the firstborn from the dead, that in all things He may have the preeminence" (Col. 1:18).

However, we must not stop there, because all of the promises of salvation in Him are found through the covenant that He made with Adam (the Adamic covenant), with Noah (the Noahic covenant), with Abraham (the Abrahamic covenant), who is called the father of our faith, with Moses (the Mosaic covenant), with Jacob (the Sini covenant), whose name was changed to Israel and from whom came all the tribes of Israel, with David (the Davidic covenant), and with what is called the new or renewed covenant instituted through Jesus Christ. We will be discussing these covenants in a later chapter as they all deal with our ancestry.

In tracing our heritage back through these individuals, one of the significant things that we must understand is the nature of "making covenant". A covenant is everlasting. Genesis 9:16 demonstrates this, "The rainbow shall be in the cloud, and I will look on it to remember the everlasting covenant between God and every living creature of all flesh that is on the earth" as does Genesis 17:7, "And I will establish My covenant between Me and you (Abraham) and your descendants after you in their generations, for an everlasting covenant, to be God to you and your descendants after you." Genesis 17:13 continues, "He who is born in your house and he who is bought with your money must be circumcised, and My covenant shall be in your flesh for an everlasting covenant." Genesis 17:19 also emphasizes the eternal nature of God's covenants, "Then God said: 'No, Sarah your wife shall bear you a son, and you shall call his name Isaac; I will establish My covenant with him for an everlasting covenant, and with his descendants after him." Psalm 105:8 reminds us, "He remembers His covenant forever, the word which He commanded, for a thousand generations."

All of the previously mentioned covenants are everlasting covenants made with those who, by faith, enter into them. Each covenant adds to the previous covenant and does not replace it, rather, it renews it. We all understand that the covenant made with Adam, stating that a Savior would come from Eve's seed, was not replaced by the covenant made with Noah, it was renewed as was Noah's covenant renewed with

Abraham and so on. Therefore, the covenant that we call the New Testament is a further renewal and is called the new or renewed covenant.

> *"Behold, the days are coming, says the* LORD, *when I will make a new covenant with the house of Israel and with the house of Judah— not according to the covenant that I made with their fathers in the day that I took them by the hand to lead them out of the land of Egypt, My covenant which they broke, though I was a husband to them, says the* LORD. *But this is the covenant that I will make with the house of Israel after those days, says the Lord: I will put My law in their minds, and write it on their hearts; and I will be their God, and they shall be My people. No more shall every man teach his neighbor, and every man his brother, saying, 'Know the* LORD,' *for they all shall know Me, from the least of them to the greatest of them, says the* LORD. *For I will forgive their iniquity, and their sin I will remember no more"* (Jer. 31:31–34).

This does not replace the Adamic covenant calling for a Savior, the seed of the woman; rather, the renewed part of this covenant makes it possible for the people of God, who had broken the former covenants, to walk out His covenant due to the renewed aspect promised here. It is a covenant made with Israel, because God chose Israel to be His nation through which He would bring salvation to all the nations of the world, according to the Abrahamic covenant. Genesis 22:18 states, "In your seed all the nations of the earth shall be blessed, because you have obeyed My voice." The Scripture makes it quite clear that due to the nature of covenant (everlasting) every renewed covenant must be made with people who are already in covenant. Jeremiah specifically tells us that this new, renewed covenant is made with Israel (Northern Kingdom) and with Judah (Southern Kingdom of Israel), thus with the whole house of Israel.

The mission and ministry of Jesus Christ (Yeshua in Hebrew), is to bring everlasting salvation to His covenant people by regathering the Northern Kingdom, who were disbursed into the nations by the Assyrians, through the preaching of the gospel to the nations of the world and reuniting the two houses of Israel, the Northern and Southern Kingdoms. If the covenant is made only with Israel, then the only way we, who are not physical descendants of Israel, can be united to Christ is by being grafted into Israel through faith in Jesus Christ. In seeking our Hebraic roots, we find that that is exactly what the Scripture says. Romans 11:19–20 demonstrates this clearly, "You will say then, 'Branches were broken off that I might be grafted in.' Well said. Because of unbelief they were broken off, and you stand by faith." Romans 11:24 continues, "For if you were cut out of the olive tree which is wild by nature, and were grafted contrary to nature into a cultivated olive tree, how much more will these, who are natural branches, be grafted into their own olive tree?"

Jesus came to save Israel according to the covenant made with Abram and his future descendants, *along with* all those who are not descended from Israel, who by faith in Jesus, can be grafted into Israel and together are the people of God. Matthew 15:24 states, "But Jesus answered and said, 'I was not sent except to the lost sheep of the house of Israel.'" Nowhere in the Bible do we find *any mention of Israel being replaced as His holy nation.* On the contrary, the promises of God made to

Israel through the covenants can never be broken by God. To do so would make God a liar.

> *"Thus says the LORD, who gives the sun for a light by day, the ordinances of the moon and the stars for a light by night, who disturbs the sea, and its waves roar (the LORD of hosts is His name): "If those ordinances depart form before Me, says the LORD, then the seed of Israel shall also cease from being a nation before me forever." Thus, says the LORD: "If heaven above can be measured, and the foundations of the earth searched out beneath, I will also cast off all the seed of Israel for all that they have done, says the LORD"* (Jer. 31:35–37).

In other words, He will never cast them off. Romans 3:3–4 shows us this, "For what if some did not believe? Will their unbelief make the faithfulness of God without effect? Certainly not! Indeed, let God be true but every man a liar." He is saying that the unfaithfulness of Israel in breaking the covenant of God will not render God unfaithful to the covenant. He will punish Israel for breaking the covenant according to the terms of the covenant, but He will not be unfaithful to fulfill His word.

In being called by God to search out our Hebraic roots, we would not be called to return to something that had been cast away, a people or a covenant. The new covenant, Jeremiah 31:31, was inaugurated when Jesus came, as recorded in the New Testament. It brings forth a 'redeemed Israel' saved by God's grace through faith. Romans 11:26–27 proclaims, "And so all Israel will be saved, as it is written: 'The Deliverer will come out of Zion, and He will turn away ungodliness from

Jacob; for this is My covenant with them, when I take away their sins."

We find that in returning to our Hebraic roots that it is really all about covenant. Within Christianity we focus so much on the New Testament writings that we almost ignore the Old Testament, regarding it as insignificant. The truth is a return to our Hebraic roots must inevitably lead us back to Abraham, Isaac, and Jacob, with whom the covenants were made, and to Moses and what took place at Mt. Sinai. Everything in the New Testament is a further revelation into these things. Jesus spoke out of the Old Testament and a part of His mission on earth was to explain these Scriptures to us, setting aside the traditions of men that had been brought along side of it. The adding of these non–biblical traditions are what the Bible calls mixed worship and it is abhorrent to the God of Israel.

The Scripture tells us in John 1:17, "For the law was given through Moses, but grace and truth came through Jesus Christ." Many teach that this verse is saying that Jesus is offering something other than the law (Torah), however what we are being told here is that Jesus came to define the Torah in such a way that the grace and truth offered in the Torah can be understood. Man's interpretation of the Torah became so distorted due to the traditions that were added to it, which are called the Oral Law. We find that salvation, through grace by faith, is first revealed in the Torah of Moses, which is God's instruction for His people given in the first five books of the Bible. His instruction hasn't changed. He does not redefine Himself or the way we are to walk before Him in the New Testament. It has always been by faith. Hebrews 11 tells us "By faith Abel [. . .] By faith Enoch [. . .] By faith Noah [. . .] By faith Abraham obeyed when he was called to go out to the place which he would receive as an inheritance." The coming of Messiah is not the first time salvation is revealed. The foundation for our salvation had already been laid through the covenants. The coming of Messiah was the enactment and the fulfillment of the promises of God contained within the covenants throughout the Old Testament. We see these promises each year through the Feasts of the Lord that were given for us to celebrate. Yes! They were given for us to celebrate. They are not Jewish feasts. They are the Feasts of the Lord for all the people of God to celebrate. That is not an opinion. It is a fact clearly written in the Word of God. Leviticus 23:2 shows this, "Speak to the children of Israel, and say to them: 'The feasts of the LORD, which you shall proclaim to be holy convocations, these are My feasts." Leviticus 23:4 continues, "These are the feasts of the LORD, holy convocations which you shall proclaim at their appointed times." Leviticus 23:37 also mentions the feasts, "These are the feasts of the Lord [. . .]" Now, if we have been grafted into Israel, which is the only way to enter into the covenants of God with Israel, then we are considered the adopted children of Israel. Romans 8:14–15 speaks of this adoption, "For as many as are led by the Spirit of God, these are sons of God. For you did not receive the spirit of bondage again to fear, but you received the Spirit of adoption by whom we cry out, 'Abba, Father.'"

One of the Feasts of the Lord, Passover, celebrates the blood of the Lamb, foreshadowing Jesus coming to earth as the Passover Lamb of God. Therefore, to return to the Hebraic roots of our faith is to return to Torah as the foundation of all that has been fulfilled. Galatians 3:24 tells us, "Therefore the law was our tutor to bring us to Christ, that we might be justified by faith." It instructs about what has been fulfilled at Christ' first coming and what has yet to be fulfilled at His second coming. The prophetic pronouncements concerning the Christ and the people of God in the Torah have not all yet been fulfilled. We must, therefore, learn to be watchmen through our study of His Word. Biblical history is also prophetic, as we shall lean when in a later chapter, we look at what is called the Greater Exodus of the last days. The plan of God laid out for us in the Old Testament and reaffirmed by Jesus in the New Testament is a plan for the restoration of all things.

> *"Repent therefore and be converted, that your sins may be blotted out, so that times of refreshing* [the Messianic era] *may come from the presence of the LORD, and that He may send Jesus Christ,* [His second coming] *who was preached to you before, whom heaven must receive until the times_of restoration of all things, which God has spoken by the mouth of all His holy prophets since the world began"* (Acts 3:19–21).

For something to be restored, it had to have existed in its original state before being corrupted.

WHY IS THE CHURCH BEING CALLED TO RETURN TO HER HEBRAIC ROOTS NOW?

The return to our Hebraic roots is related to the final phase of bringing salvation to the nations. It is through our return to these roots that we discover our true identity as the people of God. This final phase, is 'the in-gathering' of the people of God who have been scattered into the nations of the world, and who must be re-gathered in preparation of the coming of the King of Israel; the second coming of the Lord Jesus Christ to reign in the earth.

King David and his son Solomon ruled over a united Israel, all twelve tribes, the whole house of Israel. After Solomon's death, the kingdom was divided into two kingdoms, the Southern Kingdom, also known as Judah, from where we get the term "Jews", contained the tribes of Judah, Benjamin, and the half tribe of Levi. The Northern Kingdom, also known as Ephraim, Israel, and the ten tribes, began to worship idols and the Lord judged them bringing Assyria against them. They were defeated and scattered into the nations of the world, losing their identity; they became known as the ten lost tribes. Though they had abandoned the way of the Lord, He would not abandon them. Jeremiah 32:37 tells of the Lord's commitment to His people, "Behold, I will gather them out of all countries where I have driven them in My anger, in My fury, and in great wrath; I will bring them back to this place, and I will cause them to dwell safely." Joel 3:1 also highlights the Lord's promises, "For behold, in those days [the last days] and at that time when I bring back the captives of Judah and Jerusalem [. . .]"

The church has been focused on the gospel of salvation since the first coming of Messiah and has done a wonderful job of preaching that gospel, which is the declaration of the atoning blood of Christ shed on the cross for the forgiveness of sins. It has not, however, put forth the gospel of the kingdom of which the gospel of salvation is a part, in a way that incorporates the plan of God, spoken through the prophets and Jesus Himself. It is this gospel of the kingdom that I believe is the mission of the Hebraic Roots Movement. I believe that the Holy Spirit has been speaking to all within the church who will listen, to return to their Hebrew roots, to return to the church with the gospel of the kingdom. The gospel of salvation is to be preached to the world, the lost, thus to the ten lost tribes in among the nations of the world, but the gospel of the kingdom is now to be preached to the church so that they can take their place during the time of Jacob's trouble. Acts 3 does not say that all things must be restored before His return, but that the time of restoration will have begun. Not all things will be restored prior to His coming because the final things to be restored will happen during His reign in the earth. The gospel of the kingdom can only be preached to those who have received the gospel of salvation, because it must be spiritually appraised and walked out by faith. Israel will not be forgotten or abandoned. God has a plan for Israel.

I will further discuss the gospel of the kingdom in a moment, but first I want to continue with the question, "why now?" In my study of the prophetic scriptures pertaining to what the Bible calls the "time of Jacob's trouble", the tribulation period, or the last days leading up to this event I have concluded that we are living in those last days. I also believe that the emphasis on a return to the Hebraic roots of our faith and the gospel of the kingdom is, in part, the fulfillment of Daniel 12:4, "But you, Daniel, shut up the words, and seal the book until the time of the end; many shall run to and fro, and knowledge shall increase." Daniel 12:9–10 continues, "And he said, 'Go your way, Daniel, for the words are closed up and sealed till the time of the end. Many shall be purified, made white, and refined, but the wicked shall do wickedly; and none of the wicked shall understand, but the wise shall understand." I believe that it is through the return to our Hebraic roots that we will increase in knowledge and be purified, made white, and refined.

Returning now to the gospel of the kingdom, the restoration of the kingdom is always, in Scripture, referring to the kingdom of Israel. It is understood from Romans 11 that Christianity is grafted into this kingdom because of faith in Yeshua/Jesus. There are four primary aspects to be considered concerning the restoration of the Kingdom. The first is that God is going to restore the throne of David upon which Yeshua will rule in the earth. The second is that the kingdom will be restored to Israel and the world will be ruled from Jerusalem. The third is that Yeshua/Jesus will be at the center of this restoration at His second coming. The fourth is that through the restoration there will be a new heaven and a new earth.

We begin in the first book of the Bible, Genesis, where we see the need for restoration due to the sin of Adam and Eve. Genesis 3:15 highlights this need, "And I will put enmity between you and the woman, and between your seed and her Seed; He shall bruise your head and you shall bruise His heel." We understand that this is not speaking of the kingdom of Israel, because there is no Israel at this point. However, if there is no redemption of fallen mankind then restoration of the kingdom becomes irrelevant. Therefore, we see that the plan of restoration is bigger than the kingdom. However, it is through the establishment of this kingdom that the restoration of all creation, including mankind, will be accomplished by God. We can further see that this passage is speaking about the seed of the woman, and if we trace the establishment of the kingdom of Israel back to this woman, then we have the connection. The Genealogy of Jesus Christ that is found in Luke 3 does just that for us. It traces directly back to Adam and, thereby, declares Yeshua to be the seed that is spoken of in Genesis. He is then identified with the kingdom in Numbers 24:17–19:

I see Him, but not now; I behold Him, but not near; A Star shall come out of Jacob; A Scepter shall rise out of Israel, And batter the brow of Moab, And destroy all the sons of tumult [Sheth]. *"And Edom shall be a possession; Seir also, his enemies, shall be a possession, While Israel does valiantly. Out of Jacob* [Israel] *One shall have dominion, And destroy the remains of the city"* (Num. 24:17–19).

This is the prophet Balaam speaking and he is given a view into the future, "I see Him, but not now." In other words, he sees Jesus/Yeshua in the future. He says that He is going to be the king of Israel. His scepter (symbol of authority) is going to rise out of Israel, which is the scepter of a king. He is going to crush His enemies, Moab and the sons of Sheth, who are said to be the sons of disobedience.

Next, we turn to Psalm 83, a Psalm subtitled in most English Bibles as the "End of Days Conspiracy Against Israel". This gives further insight into what it was that Balaam was seeing and brings it into the present day. As I write this, the President of the United States, President Barak Obama, is said to have ordered the US ambassador to the United Nations to abstain from a vote at the Security Council. Because the United States has veto power on the UN Security Council, nothing can get passed without the support of the United States. It has been the policy of the US government for decades to veto all anti-Israel resolutions that come before the Security Council. His term will end on January 20, 2017. On January 15, 2017, there will be a meeting of seventy nations, in France, to discuss the future of Israel in time for a new proposal to be sent to the UN during President Obama's last few days as President. During that time, he can order the US ambassador to either veto such a proposal should it be put to a vote or he can order another abstention, which ultimately is a vote for the proposal. The incoming President Elect, Donald Trump has vowed that he will stand with Israel and will not allow the division of the land, however, his hands may be tied. These events, bring to mind Psalm 83.

"Do not keep silent, O God! Do not hold Your peace, and do not be still, O God! For behold, Your enemies make a tumult; and those who hate you have lifted up their head. They have taken crafty counsel against Your people, and consulted together against Your sheltered ones. They have said, 'Come, and let us cut them off from being a nation, that the name of Israel may be remembered no more.' For they have consulted together with one consent; they form a confederacy against You; the tents of Edom and the Ishmaelites; Moab and the Hagrites; Gebal, Ammon, and Amalek; Philistia with the inhabitants of Tyre; Assyria also has joined with them; they have helped the children of Lot" (Psalm 83: 1–8).

I am not suggesting that the seventy nations gathering in Paris to discuss the future of Israel is the mentioned confederacy. The Bible tells us who this confederacy is. What I am looking at is the fact that the confederacy mentioned in this passage is indeed the subject and the cause of the UN Security Council's resolutions being put forth in the first place and that they are also the main concern of those gathering in Paris. It may be that Paris has nothing to do with this at all, but it does give us pause to consider it. Psalm 83 speaks of the descendants of Esau and Ishmael and the tents of Edom and this is how it translates out today.

Tents of Edom = Palestinians & Southern Jordanians
Ishamaelites = Saudis
Moab = Palestinians & Central Jordan
Hagrites = Egyptians
Gebal = Hezbollah & North Lebanese
Ammon = Palestinians & Northern Jordanians
Amalek = Arabs of the Sinai Area
Philistia = Hamas of the Gaza Strip
Tyre = Hezbollah & Southern Lebanese
Assyria = Syrians & Northern Iraqis'

This is according to Dr. Bill Salus, featured on *Prophecy Headlines* and author of several books on last day prophesies. [1] The things that are happening in our day is cause to return to the Hebraic roots of our faith, knowing that the land of Israel and the nation of Israel are at the very center of all that God is doing in these last days. Revelation 19:7 says, "Let us be glad and rejoice and give Him glory, for the marriage of the Lamb has come, and His wife has made herself ready." We must make ourselves ready.

CHAPTER SIXTEEN

RECONSIDERING THE SABBATH

Almost everyone knows that there are ten commandments. As children, many of those who attended church learned what the Ten Commandments are, and that God gave them to Moses written on tablets of stone by the very finger of God.

THE TEN COMMANDMENTS (EX. 20:2–17, NKJV)

"You shall have no other gods before Me" (Ex. 20:3).

"You shall not make for yourself a carved image—any likeness of anything that is in heaven above, or that is in the earth beneath, or that is in the water under the earth; you shall not bow down to them nor serve them. For I, the LORD your God, am a jealous God, visiting the iniquity of the fathers upon the children to the third and fourth generations of those who hate Me, but showing mercy to thousands, to those who love Me and keep My commandments"
(Ex. 20:4–6).

"You shall not take the name of the LORD *your God in vain, for the* LORD *will not hold him guiltless who takes His name in vain"* (Ex. 20:7).

"Remember the Sabbath day, to keep it holy. Six days you shall labor and do all your work, but the seventh day is the Sabbath of the LORD *your God. In it you shall do no work: you, nor your son, nor your daughter, nor your male servant, nor your female servant, nor your cattle, nor your stranger who is within your gates. For in six days the* LORD *made the heavens and the earth, the sea, and all that is in them, and rested the seventh day. Therefore, the* LORD *blessed the Sabbath day and hallowed it"* (Ex. 20:8–11).

"Honor your father and your mother, that your days may be long upon the land which the Lord your God is giving you" (Ex. 20:12).

"You shall not murder" (Ex. 20:13).

"You shall not commit adultery" (Ex. 20:14).

"You shall not steal" (Ex. 20:15).

"You shall not bear false witness against your neighbor" (Ex. 20:16).

"You shall not covet your neighbor's house; you shall not covet your neighbor's wife, nor his male servant, nor his female servant, nor his ox, nor his donkey, nor anything that is your neighbor's" (Ex. 20:17).

The Traditional Christian Church vehemently defends the Ten Commandments as foundational to the faith. The church and the world understands that laws are necessary to the structure of any society, and for the co-existence of mankind. Human beings were not created autonomous (free to be a law to themselves) but theonomous (governed by God, subject to the law of God). The question must be asked, why does the Traditional Christian Church hold to nine of the Ten Commandments and not all ten, excluding the fourth?

MEANING OF THE WORD "SABBATH"

Baker's *Evangelical Dictionary of Biblical Theology* provides the following entry for Sabbath: "The origin of the Hebrew 'sabbat' is uncertain, but it seems to have derived from the verb 'sabat', meaning 'to stop, to cease, or to keep.' Its theological meaning is rooted in God's rest following the six days of creation." [1]

"And on the seventh day God ended His work which He had done, and He rested on the seventh day from all His work which He had done. Then God blessed the seventh day and sanctified it, because in it He rested from all His work which God had created and made" (Gen. 2:2–3).

God rested (ceased) from creating because the creation was finished. He did not need to rest from weariness.

Exodus 20:8–10 states, "Remember the Sabbath day, to keep it holy. Six days you shall labor and do all your work, but the seventh day is the Sabbath of the LORD your God. In it you shall do no work [. . .]" In this passage, we see the clear connection between the Sabbath day and the seventh day on which God the creator rested. To "remember the Sabbath day" is to acknowledge God as the creator and sustainer of the world.

The Sabbath is the seventh day and the seventh day is Saturday. How do we know this? The people of God were first commanded to keep Sabbath in the desert shortly after they left Egypt. How did they know when to keep it? In Exodus 16, we are told that during their journey in the desert, manna fell every day except for one, the Sabbath. A double portion fell on the day before the Sabbath so that they would have enough to eat for the next day as well. The people did not understand why so much manna had fallen on that day. When they came to ask Moses about this, he told them that the next day would be the Sabbath and that no manna would fall on that day. The actual wording of God's message to Moses and the Jewish people is "See! For the LORD has given you the Sabbath" (Ex. 16:29).

Deuteronomy 5:15 highlights the commandment, "And remember that you were a slave in the land of Egypt, and the Lord your God brought you out from there by a mighty hand and by an outstretched arm; therefore the Lord your God commanded you to keep the Sabbath day." Here the recognition that God is the creator of life becomes evident by the acknowledgment that He is also the savior throughout the history of His people. The "greater exodus" is a term used to describe the fulfillment of God's promise to gather His people, at the end of the age, who had been scattered into the nations of the world. This exodus out of Egypt is prophetic of the coming "greater exodus" for the people of God, from the kingdoms of this world. Therefore, to "remember the Sabbath", is to acknowledge by faith the promises of God for the future establishment of the righteous kingdom of God in the earth.

GREATER EXODUS – ISA. 11:12; EZEK. 11:17; 20:34; 36:24

The Sabbath is to be seen as a cherished gift from God, "a sign between Me and You throughout your generations" (Ex. 31:12–17) testifying of God's faithfulness to His covenant throughout the generations. The ultimate goal of the covenant promise is the establishment of His kingdom which will be a kingdom of eternal rest. Hebrews 4:9–10 reminds us, "There remains therefore a rest for the people of God. For he who has entered His rest has himself also ceased form his works as God did from His."

BIBLICAL MANDATE/COMMANDMENT

The biblical mandate concerning the Sabbath was first given by the Creator in the Genesis account, then repeated to Moses as a commandment to the people. It is not repealed anywhere in the Scripture. Authority has never been given to anyone, through sacred Scripture, to change, or to do away with, the fourth commandment.

DID JESUS CELEBRATE THE SABBATH?

First, Jesus made an emphatic statement concerning Himself and the Law, which contains the fourth commandment. In Matthew 5:17, Jesus says, "Do not think that I came to destroy the Law [Torah] or the Prophets. I did not come to destroy but to fulfill." Strong's concordance tells us that the word "destroy" is the Greek word "kataluō" and it means "to loosen, to demolish, to halt, destroy, demolish overthrow or throw down". It also reveals that the word "fulfill" is the Greek word "plēróō" and it means "to fully preach". [2] Jesus then went on to state that the Law (Torah) would continue to be relevant until heaven and earth passed away. Jesus continues in Matthew 5:18, "For assuredly, I say to you, till heaven and earth pass away, one jot or one tittle will by no means pass from the law till all is fulfilled." Strong explains, the word "fulfilled" here is the Greek word "ginōmai" and it means "be finished". [3] Jesus came to fully explain the law (Torah) to us by fully living it, because He is the living Torah. Without question, He would certainly have celebrated the Sabbath. This is evidenced several times in the New Testament (Matt. 12:1–12, Matt. 24:20, Mark 1:21, Mark 6:2, Luke 4:16–21).

WHEN WAS THE SABBATH DAY CHANGED AND BY WHOM?

It would be difficult to answer these questions adequately within the pages of this book because it requires laying out a great deal of information. It is my intention to give the reader a brief summation of the history. There are many excellent books written about the history of the church covering this issue.

SCRIPTURE

I have already provided scripture references above to show you that Jesus and His disciples celebrated the Sabbath on the seventh day, Saturday. The apostle Paul was a Torah observant Jew and continued to be so after his conversion and confession of Jesus Christ as the Messiah of the Jews and of the world, thus He continued to observe the Sabbath (Acts 13, 16, 17, 18). Many hold to the belief that the Sabbath was changed to Sunday. I contend that if the Sabbath was changed, then it could only be changed by the God who established it. Therefore, that change must be evident within the content of Scripture. Everything is to be tested by and grounded in the Scriptures.

An example of this testing can be found in Acts 17. The Old Testament was the only source available for validating what the apostle Paul was putting forth. His gospel was found to be in full agreement with the Old Testament Scriptures. It was determined that the Old Testament must be the foundation upon which the New Testament was written.

The verses that many reference concerning the Sabbath are found in Acts chapters 13, 16, and 17. These are all references to the actual Sabbath day, the seventh day of the week. Yet Acts 20:7 is a verse that many use to defend Sunday as the new Sabbath. So, let's examine this verse. To put it into context, we will look at the preceding verse as well. Acts 20:6 begins, "But we sailed away from Philippi after the Days of Unleavened Bread, and in five days joined them at Troas, where we stayed seven days." Acts 20:7 continues, "Now on the first day of the week, when the disciples came together to break bread, Paul, ready to depart the next day, spoke to them and continued his message until midnight." Verse seven states, in the English translation, that the apostles came together on the first day of the week, thus implying to many that the Sabbath was now on the first day of the week. "However, verse seven in the Greek reads 'mia ton sabbaton' which has the following meaning: 'mia=one', 'ton=of the', and 'sabbaton=Sabbaths.' The Greek word 'protos' that means 'first' is not present in this text. Therefore, the text should read, 'On one of the Sabbaths [plural] we came together to break bread', not 'On the first day [singular] of the week.' The word 'day' does not even exist in the Greek, making it even more difficult to understand the translation being 'first day of the week.'" [4]

Verse six mentions the Feast of Unleavened Bread. Unless one acknowledges the feast days that the Lord has given to us they would not understand the association between verse six, where it mentions the Feast of Unleavened Bread and verse seven where it is stated, "On one of the Sabbaths [. . .]" as pointed out within the quote above. Leviticus 23:15, instructs the people to count off seven Sabbaths after the Feast of Unleavened Bread, bringing us to the Feast of Pentecost. It is as J.N. Andrews states: "on one of the Sabbaths" after the Feast of Unleavened Bread that is being referred to here. It is not the regular Sabbath, but a high Sabbath associated with the Feast. Therefore, the people Paul was addressing were actually keeping the weekly Sabbath on the seventh day of the week and not on the first day of the week. This is just one example of a misunderstanding due to poor translation.

Almost all of the verses that are used to support changing the Sabbath day come from Paul's words. However, to consider that Paul is giving to the church an instruction that isn't rooted in the Old Testament or in the words of Messiah, is contrary to Scripture itself. For we are told in Acts 17, that the Bereans searched the Scripture (Old Testament) daily to find out whether these things that Paul was teaching them were in fact consistent with the Old Testament Scriptures and it is written, "Therefore many of them believed" (Acts 17:12). In other words, they found Paul to be true to the Scriptures.

Once again, we need to state that nowhere in Scripture is there an instruction from God that we are to no longer observe His Sabbath, or that it can be changed to be observed on another day.

J.N. Andrews declares the following concerning the Sabbath:

What a history, therefore, has the Sabbath of the Lord! It was instituted in Paradise, honored by several miracles each week for the space of forty years, proclaimed by the great Lawgiver from Sinai, observed by the Creator, the patriarchs, the prophets, the apostles, and the Son of God! It constitutes the very heart of the law of God, and so long as that law endures, so long shall the authority of this sacred institution stand fast. [5]

HISTORY

The history of the early Christian church establishes that worship services on Sunday began in Rome during the second century A.D. By the early medieval period, Sunday observance of one sort or another was quite common in the Eastern empire, as well as in the West. Samuele Bacchiocchi writes on this.

That the Church of Rome was the champion of the Sabbath fast and anxious to impose it on other Christian communities is well attested by the historical references from Bishop Callistus (A.D. 217–222), Hippolytus (c. A.D. 170–236), Pope Sylvester (A.D. 314–335), Pope Innocent I (A.D. 401–417), Augustine (A.D. 354–430), and John Cassian (c. A.D. 360–435). The fast was designed not only to express sorrow for Christ's death but also, as Pope Sylvester emphatically states: to show "contempt for the Jews" and for their Sabbat "feasting".

Bacchiocchi further points out that:

Under Vespasian (A.D. 69–79) both the Sanhedrin and the high priesthood were abolished; and under Hadrain

[. . .] the practice of the Jewish religion and particularly Sabbath keeping were outlawed. Christians were motivated to separate themselves from the Jews in the minds of the populace and rulers. They wrote against Jewish legalism and began to attack the Sabbath. Writing from Rome in about the middle of the second century, Justin Martyr condemned Sabbath observance and provided the earliest account of Christian Sunday worship services.

Christian converts from paganism tended to cling to their veneration of the Sun and, therefore, of Sunday. In early Christian art and literature, the image of the Sun was often used to represent Christ, the true "Son of righteousness."

In the earliest known Christian mosaic (dated c. A.D. 240), found below the altar of St. Peter in Rome, Christ is portrayed as the Sun (helios) ascending on the quadriga chariot with a nimbus behind His head from which irradiates seven rays in the form of a T (allusion to the cross?). Thousands of hours have been devoted to drawing the sun disk with an equal-armed cross behind the head of Christ and of other important persons.

Constantine made Sunday a civil rest day. His famous Sunday law of March 7, 321 reads as follows:

"On the venerable Day of the Sun let the magistrates and people residing in cities rest, and let all workshops be closed. In the country, however, persons engaged in agriculture may freely and lawfully continue their pursuits; because it often happens that another day is not so suitable for grain-sowing or for vine-planting; lest

by neglecting the proper moment for such operations the bounty of heaven should be lost."

The Council of Laodicea about (A.D. 364) showed respect for the Sabbath as well as Sunday, but Canon 29 provided stipulations.

"Christians shall not Judaize and be idle on Saturday but shall work on that day; but the Lord's day they shall especially honor, and, as being Christians, shall, if possible, do no work on that day. If, however, they are found Judaizing, they shall be shut out from Christ."[6]

IS THE MANDATE/COMMANDMENT FOR JEWS ONLY?

"One law shall be for the native-born and for the stranger who dwells among you" (Ex. 12:49).

The stranger who dwells among you shall be to you as one born among you, and you shall love him as yourself for you were strangers in the land of Egypt: I am the LORD your God (Lev. 19:34).

"One ordinance shall be for you of the assembly and for the stranger who dwells with you, an ordinance forever throughout your generations; as you are, so shall the stranger be before the LORD. One law and one custom shall be for you and for the stranger who dwells with you" (Num. 15:15–16).

We can see form the passages above that whosoever worshiped the God of Israel was to worship as the people of

Israel worshiped. There was to be no mixed worship. He would be worshiped only according to His instructions. An even more tremendous reality is declared by the Apostle Paul in the following passages.

> *And if some of the branches were broken off, and you, being a wild olive tree, were grafted in among them, and with them became a partaker of the root and fatness of the olive tree [. . .]* (Rom. 11:17).

> *For you are all sons of God through faith in Christ Jesus. For as many of you as were baptized into Christ have put on Christ. There is neither Jew nor Greek, there is neither slave nor free, there is neither male nor female; for you are all one in Christ Jesus. And if you are Christ's, then you are Abraham's seed and, heirs according to the promise* (Gal. 3:26–29).

Therefore, the answer to the above question is emphatically no! According to the above Scriptures, we can clearly see that this commandment is for all who worship the God of Israel, Jews and non-Jewish believers alike. We must also remember the words of Leviticus 19:34, "The stranger who dwells among you shall be as one born among you [. . .]"

GOD'S CONTINUED PROCLAMATION BY THE PROPHETS

For the prophets, who were the mouthpiece of God to the people, the Sabbath was the standard for Israel's obedience to its covenant with God. We can see several examples of this throughout Scripture. Several of these passages have been highlighted below and additional Scripture concerning the Sabbath can be found in Isaiah 6:23, Ezekiel 20:13–26, Ezekiel 23:38, Ezekiel 44:24, and Ezekiel 46:1.

ISAIAH CONCERNING THE FUTURE OF JERUSALEM – ISA. 58:13–14

If you turn away your foot from the Sabbath, from doing your pleasure on My holy day, and call the Sabbath a delight, the holy day of the LORD honorable, and shall honor Him, not doing your own ways, nor finding your own pleasure, nor speaking your own words, then you shall delight yourself in the LORD; and I will cause you to ride on the high hills of the earth, and feed you with the heritage of Jacob your father. The mouth of the LORD has spoken (Isa. 58:13–14).

ISAIAH CONCERNING THE PEOPLE OF GOD – ISA. 56:2

"Blessed is the man who does this, and the son of man who lays hold on it; who keeps from defiling the Sabbath, and keeps his hand from doing any evil" (Isa. 56:2).

Those who honor the day will find delight in the Lord, riding on the heights of the earth and being fed with the heritage of Jacob. Isaiah 58:14 demonstrates this, "Then you shall delight yourself in the LORD; and I will cause you to ride on the high hills of the earth, and feed you with the heritage of Jacob your father. The mouth of the LORD has spoken."

EZEKIEL CONCERNING ISRAEL – EZEK. 20:12–14

"Moreover I also gave them My Sabbaths, to be a sign between them and Me, that they might know that I am the LORD who sanctifies them. Yet the house of Israel rebelled against Me in the wilderness; they did not walk in My statutes; they despised My judgments, which, if a man does, he shall live by them; and they greatly defiled My Sabbaths. Then I said I would pour out My fury on them in the wilderness, to consume them. But I acted for My name's sake, that it should not be profaned before the Gentiles, in whose sight I had brought them out" (Ezek. 20:12–14).

AMOS ON THE ATTITUDE OF THE PEOPLE – AMOS 8:5

"When will the New Moon be past, that we may sell grain? And the Sabbath, that we may trade wheat [. . .]" (Amos 8:5).

WHY IS THIS ISSUE ARISING TODAY?

I believe that this issue, along with many other doctrinal issues, are arising today due to the times in which we live. Acts 3:20–21 tells us the following, "[. . .] and that He may send Jesus Christ, who was preached to you before, whom heaven must receive until the times of restoration of all things, which God has spoken by the mouth of all His holy prophets since the world began." I believe that the issue of the Sabbath, the reinstitution of the Fourth Commandment to the people of God, is one among those things that are to be restored prior to the second coming of the Lord.

I also believe that when the prophet Daniel was speaking of "the time of the end" (Dan. 12:4) that he was speaking of our day and of the times of restoration of all things. Daniel 12:4 states, "But you, Daniel, shut up the words, and seal the book until the time of the end; many shall run to and fro, and knowledge shall increase." Later on in the text we read, "And he said, 'Go your way, Daniel, for the words are closed up and sealed till the time of the end. Many shall be purified, made white, and refined, but the wicked shall do wickedly; and none of the wicked shall understand, but the wise shall understand" (Dan. 12:9–10). As stated by Living Word Ministries, "We live in some of the most exciting days in human history! One only has to read the newspapers or listen to the news daily to see prophecy being fulfilled. At the same time, Christians around the world are engaging in quests to restore the foundations of their faith, that is the Hebraic faith of Yeshua (Jesus). The movement to restore the Hebrew Roots of Christianity is exploding." [7]

According to Dr. John Garr, publisher of *Restore Magazine*, "This reawakening is occurring independently in the lives of believers throughout the world. It is bringing the restoration of the knowledge, practice and study of the biblical, Hebraic roots of Christianity into the faith. This renewed interest in the Hebrew roots of Christianity is one of the greatest and most universal works that the Holly Spirit is producing in the church in this generation. This is affecting the way growing numbers of Christians throughout the world are thinking and acting about their families, their community life, their church relationships, and, most importantly, their relationship with the God of the Bible." [8]

Dr. Robert D. Heidler, author of *The Messianic Church Arising!*, states, "The Church is rising up in power and glory that we have not seen since the first century. Jesus is preparing His Bride. The Holy Spirit of God is restoring the covenant roots of His Church."[9]

I sincerely hope that this has helped you to understand more about the Fourth Commandment, the Sabbath of God. I encourage you to be willing to reconsider not only the Sabbath, but that you would, "Test all things; hold fast what is good" (1 Thess. 5:21). Remember the words of John 17:16–17, "They are not of the world, just as I am not of the world. Sanctify them by Your truth. Your word is truth."

CHAPTER SEVENTEEN

THE FEAST
OF THE LORD

The very next thing that the Lord began to lead us to study were the Feasts of the Lord. We had never considered, had never even heard the term "Celebrating Jesus in the Feast" until, as I said, I met Dr. Booker at the prophetic conference in Florida. We were intrigued and dove into the study of these feasts with great zeal. The real challenge was not so much in understanding what the Holy Spirit was teaching us concerning the feast as trying to figure out how to celebrate them. Fortunately, we had two Jewish women in our congregation who had been raised in Jewish Orthodox homes, celebrating the feasts each year. One of these women had also been celebrating Jesus in the feast for several years, having to travel great distances to do so. They were both very helpful in our understanding as to how to go about it all. The following is a brief account of the knowledge our study provided us with. This too became a part of our holy conversation.

WHAT IS A BIBLICAL FEAST?

In order for us to understand what a biblical feast is, we need to go back to the original language, the Hebrew language. The word most often translated as "feast" in English is the Hebrew word "châgag" (pronounced khaw-gag') and it means "to march in a sacred procession, to observe a festival; by implication to be giddy—celebrate, dance, (keep, hold) a (solemn) feast (holiday), reel to and fro."[1] In other words, it is to be a delightful celebration. But what is it a celebration of? Each of the feasts is a celebration of a specific historical event, prophesied future event, or both. All of the feasts are celebrations of the interaction of Yahweh, the God of Abraham, Isaac, and Jacob/Israel, and His people. They reflect the promises and oaths made by Yahweh through covenants and the fulfillment of those covenant promises by Yeshua/Jesus the Messiah. The English word "feast" is also translated from another Hebrew word "mô 'êd" (pronounced mo-ade); its meaning is "an appointment, i.e. a fixed time or season; (specifically) a festival; an assembly convened for a definite purpose; a place of solemn assembly, congregation."[2]

WHAT HAVE WE TO DO WITH THE BIBLICAL FEASTS TODAY?

Like the celebration of the Sabbath, which is a feast as well, the biblical feasts were removed from Christianity for reasons too numerous and involved to get into here, among which were their identification with the Jews. There are many good books available on the history of Christianity that detail this departure. Theologically, it is misstated that the feasts were all fulfilled in Yeshua at the cross and have therefore no significance any longer. It is, however, a partially true statement. Some of the feasts had a partial fulfillment with Yeshua's death, burial, and resurrection as we shall see further on in this book. Suffice it to say that like the Sabbath, the feasts were given by

Yahweh to be everlasting celebrations. We are instructed in the Bible to keep/celebrate these feasts throughout all generations. The celebration of the Sabbath is a sign between Yahweh and His covenant people (Ex. 31:13) and the celebration of the feasts is an expression of faith in Yahweh and a continual acknowledgment that we are in covenant with the God of our salvation. Each time we celebrate these feasts it serves as a reminder of what Yahweh has done, is doing, and is yet to do.

WHOSE FEASTS ARE THEY REALLY?

Once again, through Christianity's attempt to isolate itself from Judaism, it has replaced these feasts with other feast or holy days. It has, therefore, labeled these biblical feasts as Jewish feasts. Within the traditional church, if we had ever even heard of these feasts, believed them to be Jewish feasts. The Jews, being non-Christian, therefore rendered their feasts non-Christian. However, according to the Bible, these feasts are not Jewish feasts although they were given to all believers in Yahweh through the Jewish people. Leviticus 23:1–2 tells us, "And the LORD spoke to Moses, saying, 'Speak to the children of Israel, and say to them: The feasts of the LORD, which you shall proclaim to be holy convocations, these are My feasts." The English word "convocations" here is the Hebrew word "miqrâ'" (pronounced mik-raw) and it means "something called out, i.e. a public meeting; also a rehearsal:--assembly, calling, convocation, reading." [3] This tells us that the feasts are not only a celebration, but also a rehearsal for something that is yet to happen that we will have participation in. We are to be rehearsed and ready for that participation. These are not the Jews feasts, they are not the Christians feasts, they are the feasts of the Lord, "these are My feasts."

When we understand that as Christians we have been "grafted into Israel" (Rom. 11, Eph. 2), then we understand that these feasts, which are in fact the feasts of the God of Israel, must be celebrated by the Christian church. We are grafted into Israel and are therefore Israelites. We are not, nor can we ever become Jews. Only those who are born Jews are Jews, but we do become a part of the kingdom of God whose kingdom is Israel.

HOW MANY FEASTS ARE THERE?

There are seven feasts of the Lord. There are four feasts celebrated in the spring and three in the fall. Leviticus 23:4 tells us, "These are the feasts of the LORD, holy convocations which you shall proclaim at their appointed times." Leviticus 23:5 continues, "On the fourteenth day of the first month at twilight is the LORD's Passover."

The first of the spring feasts is the Feast of Passover, in Hebrew it is called Pesach. It is celebrated in the Hebrew month of Nissan, which begins in our month of April and concludes in our month of May. For example, in the year 2016, Nissan first began on April ninth and the month ended on May eighth, making it a thirty-day month. Passover is an eight-day feast. Leviticus 23:6 marks the time for the Feast of Passover, "And on the fifteenth day of the same month is the Feast of Unleavened Bread to the LORD; seven days you must eat unleavened bread."

The second of the spring feasts is the Feast of Unleavened Bread, which in Hebrew is called "Matzot". This feast begins on the second day of Passover and is a seven-day feast also occurring in the month of Nissan.

"Speak to the children of Israel, and say to them: 'When you come into the land which I give to you, and reap its harvest, then you shall bring a sheaf of the firstfruits of your harvest to the priest. He shall wave the sheaf before the LORD, to be accepted on your behalf; on the day after the Sabbath the priest shall wave it'" (Lev. 23:10–11).

The third of the spring feasts is the Feast of Firstfruits, which in Hebrew is called Yom HaBikkurim. This feast occurs on the first Sunday, "from the day after the Sabbath [. . .]" (Lev. 23:15) after the Feast of Unleavened Bread. It is a one day feast. However, it begins the Feast of Weeks leading up to the Feast of Pentecost. Leviticus 23:14–16 describes this event.

"[. . .] it shall be a statute forever throughout your generations in all your dwellings. And you shall count for yourselves from the day after the Sabbath, from the day that you brought the sheaf of the wave offering: seven Sabbaths shall be completed. Count fifty days [Feast of Weeks/ Counting of the Omer] *to the day after the seventh Sabbath; then you shall offer a new grain offering to the Lord"* (Lev. 23:14–16).

The fourth of the spring feasts is the Feasts of Pentecost, which in Hebrew is called Shavuot. This feast occurs during the summer, however, it is often joined with the spring feasts and identified as a part of that grouping. This feast occurs fifty days after the Feast of Firstfruits, on the Sunday following the seventh Sabbath after Firstfruits. This is what is being referred to in Acts 20:7, which was mentioned earlier. It occurs during the Hebrew month of Sivan, the month of June. The next grouping of feasts are what is referred to as the fall feasts. There are three fall feasts.

> *Then the LORD spoke to Moses, saying, "Speak to the children of Israel, saying: 'In the seventh month, on the first day of the month, you shall have a sabbath-rest, a memorial of blowing of trumpets, a holy convocation'"* (Lev. 23:23–24).

The first of the fall feasts and the fifth Feast of the Lord is the Feast of Trumpets, in Hebrew it is called Rosh Hashanah or Yom Teruah. It is also called the new year. This feast occurs in the month of Tishrei, our month of October, and is a one day feast.

Lev. 23:26–27 speaks of the sixth feast, "And the Lord spoke to Moses, saying: 'Also the tenth day of this seventh month shall be the Day of Atonement. It shall be a holy convocation for you [. . .]'" The second of the fall feasts and the sixth Feast of the Lord is the Feast of Atonement, in Hebrew it is called Yom Kippur. It is to be celebrated on the tenth day of Tishrei, our month of October. Leviticus 23:31 speaks about the eternal nature of the feasts, "[. . .] it shall be a statute forever throughout your generations in all your dwellings."

Leviticus 23:33–34 states, "Then the Lord spoke to Moses, saying, 'Speak to the children of Israel, saying: The fifteenth day of this seventh month shall be the Feast of Tabernacles for seven days to the LORD." The third of the fall feasts and the seventh Feast of the Lord is the Feast of Tabernacles, which in Hebrew is called Sukkot. It occurs in the month of Tishrei or October. This is a seven-day feast with a holy convocation on the eight day.

DEFINITION OF A HIGH SABBATH

There are times when these feasts fall on a weekly Sabbath day, however, when they do not fall on the weekly Sabbath day and there is a "holy convocation" called for within the feast, then that day becomes as a Sabbath day and is to be celebrated as such. There are times when there are two days set aside within a feast, in addition to a weekly Sabbath day, and those days are specifically cited within the instruction given to Moses for the people. For example, the Feast of Tabernacles calls for a holy convocation on the first and eighth day of the feast, in addition to the weekly Sabbath.

WHAT IS THE PURPOSE OF THE FEASTS?

As I said earlier, the purpose of the feasts can be found in the Hebrew words associated with the feasts. Primarily the feasts are to celebrate Yahweh and His interaction with His people. The songs of the feasts celebrate the great deeds of the God of Israel, such as delivering them from Egypt with a mighty hand and so on. These celebrations stir within the people the faith to continue to reach out to Yahweh with a current hope in whatever situation they find themselves in: throughout times of war, times of captivity, times of greatness, through trials, tribulation, and so on. It is still so today. Those who celebrate the Feasts of the Lord today are renewed by them.

I have seen that the Feasts of the Lord were given to be celebrated as an everlasting memorial for every generation. They are everlasting feasts. They are a historical record of God's faithfulness and until all is fulfilled, they are the prophetic blueprint for the future. We celebrate the feasts today out of obedience to the Lord and as an expression of faith in Him, a faith that responds to His commands as fidelity. We celebrate the Feasts of the Lord today in order to understand the prophetic significance of each feast and to rehearse for the day when these prophetic events are to take place.

HOW DOES THE CELEBRATION OF THE FEASTS HONOR GOD?

First and foremost, the celebration of the feasts honor God because we are obedient to do what He has instructed through His prophet Moses. Second, through obedience comes the blessings of God, which brings glory to His name. The world rejoices over the expression of a loving God's blessings upon His people due to their obedience. So long as Israel obeyed Yahweh, through His blessing upon them, they became a shining city on a hill for the whole world to see, just as Yeshua said we were to continue to be (Matt. 5:14). Third, we honor God by becoming watchmen on the wall as told in Isaiah 62:6, "I have set watchmen on your walls, O Jerusalem; they shall never hold their peace day or night. You who make mention of the LORD, do not keep silent [. . .]" The prophet Isaiah heard the Lord in Isaiah 6:8 saying, "Whom shall I send, and who will go for Us?" When we celebrate the Feasts of the Lord we are rehearsing, as we look for the signs of the fulfillment of these feasts. We are brought back in order to look forward. Just as there was a Passover in the first Exodus, there will be a Passover in the greater Exodus that is to come. With greater insight gained by studying the feasts, we are to judge world affairs considering the prophetic meaning of the feasts so that we can be watchmen on the wall, warning the people as events unfold. Yeshua, when speaking of the things to come in Matthew 24, is speaking the language of the feasts and their prophetic meaning. In Matthew 24:42, he said, "Watch therefore". In Matthew 24:44 he concludes, "Therefore you also be ready."

Celebrating the Feasts of the Lord honors God because we are exercising our faith in Him to do just what He says He will do; to bring us into and through the fullness of redemption. The celebration is the expression of that faith and proves the Word of God in us. My faith is not dead, for you can see my faith by my good works (James 2:14), works for which I was created (Eph. 2:10). The works for which we were created certainly include the celebration of the everlasting Feasts of the Lord.

DID YESHUA/JESUS CELEBRATE THE FEASTS WHILE ON EARTH?

Yeshua was raised by Jewish parents, studied in the Tanakh/ Old Testament, and as a young man became a Jewish Rabbi/ teacher. He certainly would have celebrated all the Feasts of the Lord. They were after all His feasts. He was the Incarnate God of Israel. What Christianity calls the Last Supper, was actually a celebration of the Passover Meal.

Then came the Day of Unleavened Bread, when the Passover must be killed. And He sent Peter and John, saying, "Go and prepare the Passover for us, that we may eat." So they said to Him, "Where do You want us to prepare?" And He said to them, "Behold, when you have entered the city, a man will meet you carrying a pitcher of water; follow him into the house which he enters. Then you shall say to the master of the house, 'The Teacher [Rabbi] says to you, "Where is the guest room where I may eat the Passover with My disciples?"' Then he will show you a large, furnished upper room; there make ready." So they went and found it just as He had said to them, and they prepared the Passover. When the hour had come, He sat down, and the twelve apostles with Him. Then He said to them "With fervent desire I have desired to eat this Passover with you before I suffer; for I say to you, I will no longer eat of it until it is fulfilled in the kingdom of God" (Luke 22: 7–16).

In 1 Corinthians 5:7, The apostle Paul says, "For indeed Christ, our Passover, was sacrificed for us [. . .]" We understand that Yeshua/Jesus is the Passover Lamb and partially fulfilled this feast of Passover. In the verse above, He tells His disciples that "I will no longer eat of it *until it is fulfilled* in the kingdom of God" (emphasis mine). Thus, telling us that there is still a future fulfillment and a future celebration of this feast.

HAVE ANY OF THE FEASTS ACTUALLY BEEN FULFILLED?

When we, as Christians, talk about celebrating Yeshua/Jesus in the feasts, we are speaking of celebrating Him in those feasts that were partially fulfilled during His earthly ministry. As the Passover Lamb who was slain, His blood can be applied to cleanse us from sin (Heb. 9:14). However, the Passover is not completely fulfilled until that blood is applied to every heart that is to be a part of the kingdom of God, both of Jews who are regrafted in to Israel and those non-Jews who are grafted in by faith in Yeshua. Passover is also not completely fulfilled until we have all crossed over into the promised land, the Millennial Reign of Christ at the end of the age, when peace shall reign throughout the earth and the kingdom of God rules and reigns over all kingdoms in the earth.

Yeshua/Jesus fulfilled the Feast of Unleavened Bread in that He is the Bread of Life that came down from heaven (John 6:51). Leaven is often a metaphor for sin and He had no sin in Him and was therefore the only one who could fulfill this feast. However, once again He became unleavened bread for us so that we might all become unleavened, without sin.

> *"Therefore purge out the old leaven, that you may be a new lump, since you truly are unleavened. For indeed Christ, our Passover, was sacrificed for us. Therefore, let us keep the feast, not with old leaven, nor with the leaven of malice and wickedness, but with the unleavened bread of sincerity and truth"* (1 Cor. 5:7–8).

There is still a purging work that is taking place as a part of the fulfillment of this feast. This purging is the work of the Holy Spirit called sanctification in which we cooperate with the Holy Spirit.

> *"Therefore, my beloved, as you have always obeyed, not as in my presence only, but now much more in my absence, work out your own salvation with fear and trembling; for it is God who works in you both to will and to do for His good pleasure"* (Phil. 2:12–13).

Yeshua/Jesus fulfilled the Feast of Firstfruits in that He was the first to rise from the dead and to be presented to the Father. However, the firstfruits represent the whole harvest and the whole harvest will not be presented to the Father until the end of the age when the completeness of this fulfillment occurs. We, who believe in Messiah, are all a part of that harvest (Matt. 13:37–43).

On the day of Pentecost, the Holy Spirit was given as was promised by Messiah and will continue to be given until the end of the age. Acts 2:39 says, "For the promise is to you and to your children, and to all who are afar off, as many as the Lord our God will call."

Therefore, that grouping called the spring feasts all have their place in history and were to some extent fulfilled by Christ. This is just as the fall feasts will be fulfilled by Christ at the appointed time. All of these feasts are tied to the restoration of all things.

But those things which God foretold by the mouth of all His prophets, that the Christ would suffer, He has thus fulfilled. Repent therefore and be converted, that your sins may be blotted out, so that times of refreshing may come from the presence of the Lord, and that He may send Jesus Christ, who was preached to you before, whom heaven must receive until the times of restoration of all things, which God has spoken by the mouth of all His holy prophets since the world began (Acts 3:18–21).

CHAPTER EIGHTEEN

THE
EVERLASTING COVENANTS

When reading the Bible, most people think in terms of testaments, the Old and New Testaments. We have not given much thought to the covenants that are found within the pages of the Bible. When we consider the word "testament" we think of things like a last will and testament, which we know is done away with once one of the parties of the testament dies. Therefore, it would be logical to believe that, with the coming of the New Testament, the Old Testament was made null and void upon the death of Yeshua/Jesus. Many of us have concluded that the Old Testament does not hold much value in directing our lives. We believed that the laws and precepts of the New Testament contain all we need to live righteously before God.

The Bible itself declares that it is based upon the covenants that God has made with man and it does not recognize a testament as the basis for relationship with God. Whereas, a testament is terminated upon the death of one of the parties, a covenant is everlasting. Genesis 17:7 speaks of the everlasting nature of covenants, "And I will establish My covenant between Me and you and your descendants after you in their generations, for an everlasting covenant, to be God to you and your descendants after you." Covenants are also different than contracts. Many people view covenants as some sort of bargained agreements involving the exchange of consideration. While there are some similarities between contracts and covenants, the covenant goes far deeper and extends beyond the bounds of a contract.

Fausset's Bible Dictionary gives the following definition for covenant, "Covenant involves a stipulation of something to be done by the person offering the covenant, there is a restipulation by the other party of something to be done or given in consideration which constitutes acceptance and which forms the essence of the agreement. Finally, there must be some penalty to the party that violates the agreements. The notion of a covenant in the strict sense, as requiring two independent contracting parties, cannot apply to a covenant between (Elohim) God and man. His covenant must be essentially one of gratuitous promise, an act of pure grace on His part. So, in Psalm 89:28 'covenant' is explained by the parallel word 'mercy'". [1] Notice that this definition makes a distinction between covenants involving men and a covenant made with God.

A testament or a contract can be altered, changed or ended and a new one established, whereas, an everlasting covenant cannot. An everlasting covenant can be added to in order to renew it, as in the case of the Sinai or Mosaic covenant which is added to the Abrahamic covenant of promise. These covenants are everlasting covenants and are distinguished from each other by what is added, in this case the instruction given through Torah.

In a similar way, what we call the New Testament is biblically referred to as the new, or more appropriately, the renewed covenant. The Abrahamic covenant of promise is mentioned approximately one hundred times in the New Testament. It is not testament language, but covenant language that is spoken in the Scriptures. Just as a marriage covenant is meant to be an 'until death do us part,' the biblical covenants are meant to continue throughout our lives. It is also given for each generation that follows. Because these covenants are made with a God who is everlasting, they extend beyond death and into eternal life for those who keep covenant. Since the everlasting covenants made with the fathers, Abraham, Isaac, and Jacob/Israel, apply to our generation, then it is of great importance that we understand the covenants.

TYPES OF COVENANTS

There are two types of covenants in the Bible, conditional and unconditional. There are eight covenants when the Land covenant is considered separately from the Abrahamic covenant. This is often the case, especially today since the land of Israel is being highly contested.

CONDITIONAL COVENANTS

A conditional covenant is a bilateral (two party) covenant. Within this covenant, God promises to do something if the people will do something. In other words, if you will do this, then I will do this. God promises blessings if man fulfills his part of the covenant. God proclaims curses if man does not fulfill his part. There are two conditional covenants in the Bible, the Edenic covenant and the Mosaic covenant.

UNCONDITIONAL COVENANTS

An unconditional covenant is a unilateral (one-sided) covenant. God establishes this covenant and promises blessing for His covenant people. He unconditionally promises blessings. This is a grace covenant. He gives unmerited favor to the people. He is glorified through the blessing upon His people. These covenants are everlasting throughout all generations. God will fulfill them. Unconditional covenants were made only with the nation of Israel (Rom. 9:4), which includes all who are grafted into the nation (Rom. 11; Eph. 2:11–22).

THE EDENIC COVENANT – GEN. 1:28–30, GEN. 2:15–17, HOS. 6:7

This is a covenant that was made between God and Adam. Adam is what, in theology, is called the Federal Head, meaning that he stood as the representative head of humanity. That is why the actions of Adam are attributed to the whole of humanity. The following is contained in the Edenic Covenant:

"Be fruitful and multiply" (Gen. 1:28)
"Subdue" the earth (Gen. 1:28)
Man was given "dominion" over all living things (Gen. 1:28)
"Tend and keep" the garden (Gen. 2:15)
"And the LORD God commanded the man, saying, 'Of every tree of the garden you may freely eat; but of the tree of the knowledge of good and evil you shall not eat [. . .]" (Gen. 2:16–17)

THE ADAMIC COVENANT – GEN. 3:14–19

Once again, this covenant is made between God and Adam. Adam again is the Federal Head of the human race, therefore, the judgment on Adam is a judgment on the whole human race. We find the first prophecy within the provisions of this covenant. It is the prophecy of the Lord's victory over Satan as we are told that the woman's Seed would crush Satan's head (Gen. 3:15). The Adamic covenant is an unconditional covenant. One of the provisions of this covenant has to do with the conscience of man.

For the wrath of God is revealed from heaven against all ungodliness and unrighteousness of men, who suppress the truth in unrighteousness, because what may be known of God is manifest in them, for God has shown it to them. For since the creation of the world His invisible attributes are clearly seen, being understood by the things that are made, even His eternal power and Godhead, so that they are without excuse, because, although they knew God, they did not glorify Him as God, nor were thankful, but became futile in their thoughts, and their foolish hearts were darkened (Rom. 1:18–21).

From this passage, we see this covenant is still upheld in Paul's day and today.

THE NOAHIC COVENANT

This covenant was made between God and Noah. With the exception of Noah's family (eight people) the entire human race was destroyed. Genesis 6:5 proclaimed, "[. . .] the wickedness of man was great in the earth." All of the nations of the world would come forth from this one family. Just as with the Edenic Covenant, man was commissioned to repopulate the earth.

The promise contained within this covenant is that God would never again destroy mankind with a flood (Gen. 9:9–11). With this covenant, the governance of man by man and the rule of law were ordained. Capital punishment is introduced for the first time. Human government began under this covenant and it is the violation of this everlasting covenant (Gen. 9:16), that brings the judgement upon humanity during the Tribulation period (Isa. 24:5–6).

THE ABRAHAMIC COVENANT – GEN. 12:1–3, GEN. 7, GEN. 13:14–17, GEN. 15:1–22, GEN. 22:15–18

There are many things to consider within this covenant.

Abraham would become a great nation (Gen. 12:2).
He is promised land (Gen. 12:7).
He was to be greatly blessed (Gen. 12:2).
His name would be great (Gen. 12:2).
He would be a blessing to others (Gen. 12:2).
Those who bless Israel will be blessed (Gen. 12:3).
In him all nations would be blessed (Gen. 22:18).
He would receive a son through his wife Sarah (Gen. 15:1–4).
His descendants would go into bondage (Gen. 15:13–14).
Other nations would come forth from him through Isaac (Gen. 17:3–4,6)

The ultimate fulfillment of the Abrahamic covenant will take place during the Messianic Era and is therefore evidence that it is an everlasting covenant.

THE COVENANT WITH JACOB/ISRAEL

One of the most important covenants God made was with the Israelites, Abraham's descendants through his son Isaac and grandson Jacob (renamed Israel). The apostle Paul speaks about who the Israelites are.

> [. . .] *who are Israelites, to whom pertain the adoption, the glory, the covenants, the giving of the law, the service of God, and the promises; of whom are the fathers and from who, according to the flesh, Christ came, who is over all, the eternally blessed God. Amen.* (Rom. 9:4–5).

This covenant with Israel, sometimes referred to as the Land covenant, is essential to the state of Israel today as it is the basis for their claim on the land in which they now reside.

> *Then God appeared to Jacob again, when he came from Padan Aram, and blessed him. And God said to him, "Your name is Jacob; your name shall not be called Jacob anymore, but Israel shall be your name." So He called his name Israel. Also God said to him: "I am God Almighty. Be fruitful and multiply; a nation and a company of nations shall proceed from you, and kings shall come from your body. The land which I gave Abraham and Isaac I give to you; and to your descendants after you I give this land"* (Gen. 35:9–12).

THE MOSAIC COVENANT – EX. 20

This was a renewal of the Abrahamic Covenant, a covenant which was made with Moses and the people at Mt. Sinai. The Torah was the content of this covenant which provided guidelines for living in the Abrahamic covenant. It was given to teach the people how to live in the promises made to Abraham and his descendants. A person becomes spiritually alive (born again) through the renewed Abrahamic covenant by faith, and the Mosaic covenant teaches him how to live that new life in God. Galatians 3:10–23 clearly states that no one is justified by the Torah alone, for the righteous shall live by and be justified by faith, just as Abraham was. Abraham believed God and it was reckoned to him as righteousness. The Torah does not impart life to sinners, it is life for those already alive. To live out our faith is to live a life in obedience to the Word of God (Torah) by the Mosaic covenant. The Torah defines the covenant lifestyle.

THE DAVIDIC COVENANT – 2 SAM. 7

"When your days are fulfilled and you rest with your fathers, I will set up your seed after you, who will come from your body, and I will establish his kingdom. He shall build a house for My name, and I will establish the throne of his kingdom forever" (2 Sam. 7:12–13).

It will be an eternal kingdom. In 2 Samuel 7, King David decided that he wanted to build a house for God. He shares this desire with the prophet Nathan. Elohim (God) sends a word to Nathan that David is not to build this house but "his Son" will build the house. We know that David's son, Solomon, did build what is known as Solomon's Temple. However, as is often the case, there is a deeper meaning here referring to the seed of David, the Messiah Yeshua (Jesus) who will build the house of God. The fulfillment of the Davidic covenant awaits the second coming of Messiah King, who will build and establish an eternal kingdom/house. We must keep in mind that the Davidic covenant is an extension of all the covenants before it and includes the conditions of those covenants for blessing or cursing. 1 Peter 2:5 says, "[. . .] you also, as living stones, are being built up a spiritual house, a holy priesthood, to offer up spiritual sacrifices acceptable to God through Jesus Christ."

THE NEW/RENEWED COVENANT

"Behold the days are coming, says the LORD, when I will make a new covenant with the house of Israel and with the house of Judah—not according to the covenant I made with their fathers in the day that I took them by the hand to lead them out of the land of Egypt, My covenant which they broke, though I was a husband to them, says the LORD. But this is the covenant that I will make with the house of Israel after those days, says the LORD: I will put My law [Torah] in their minds, and write it on their hearts; and I will be their God, and they shall be My people. *No more shall every man teach his neighbor, and every man his brother, saying 'Know the LORD,' for they all shall know Me, from the least of them to the greatest of them says the LORD. For I will forgive their iniquity, and their sin I will remember no more"* (Jer. 31:31–34).

What Christianity knows as the New covenant or the New Testament is in fact a further fulfillment of the everlasting covenants that preceded it. That is one reason why the Abrahamic covenant is mentioned approximately one hundred times in the New Testament.

We are now going to look at the different kinds of covenants trying to determine what they mean to us today and what we can learn from them. There are four kinds of covenants that we read about in the Scriptures. They are the Blood Covenant, the Salt Covenant, the Sandal Covenant and the Betrothal Covenant.

BLOOD COVENANT

The first type of covenant is called a blood covenant. The Adamic covenant and the Noahic covenant were both blood covenants. Through this type of covenant, we enter into a relationship of servanthood. This covenant requires the shedding of blood. We walk in this covenant and become servants of the living God and renew this covenant with Him each day as we confess our sins and plead the blood of the covenant (Yeshua's blood) for the forgiveness of our sins, so that we might continue to serve Him faithfully. Ephesians 6:6 tells us, "[. . .] but as bondservants of Christ, doing the will of God from the heart [. . .]"

SALT COVENANT

The salt covenant is also called the covenant of friendship. A friendship covenant involves commitment. When we enter into the salt covenant with God, He adds the element of friendship to the servant (blood) covenant. This addition illustrates the cumulative nature of covenant. John 15:15 demonstrates this, "No longer do I call you servants, for a servant does not know what his master is doing; but I have called you friends, for all things that I heard from My Father I have made known to you." It was not that they would no longer serve Him. Rather, it was to assure them of a closer relationship with them during their service. They were about to enter into their greatest service by being His witnesses, even unto death. We as Christians rely heavily upon this relationship with our Lord and Savior. To suggest that this covenant is not everlasting, and that we do not walk in this covenant but are only servants, would be to diminish the words of Yeshua. In John 17:21 he says,

"[. . .] that they all may be one, as You, Father, are in Me, and I in You; that they also may be one in Us [. . .]"

SANDAL COVENANT

The sandal covenant is also called an inheritance covenant. Sandals were used to represent the inheritance concept. The ancient Hebrews used worn-out sandals to mark the boundaries of their property. They partially covered them with rocks to hold them in place against the natural elements. God had told them that where ever your feet shall tread shall be yours forever (Deut. 11:24). An example of this is found in the book of Ruth. In Ruth 4:1–13 we see how the closest relative of Ruth chose not to purchase her family's field, nor to take her as his wife. Instead, he allowed Ruth's cousin Boaz to acquire both the land, Ruth, and yielded up his right to possess by removing his sandal and handing it to Boaz.

The sandal covenant is a picture of the relationship of sons and daughters with their parents. Colossians 3:23–24 speaks of inheritance, "And whatever you do, do it heartily, as to the Lord and not to men, knowing that from the Lord you will receive the reward of the inheritance; for you serve the Lord Christ." This passage ties the servant to the inheritance because we, as heirs, are to be good stewards over the inheritance.

> *For as many as are led by the Spirit of God, these are sons of God. For you did not receive the spirit of bondage again to fear, but you received the Spirit of adoption by whom we cry out, "Abba, Father." The Spirit Himself bears witness with our spirit that we are children of God, and if children, then heirs—heirs of God and joint heirs with Christ, if indeed we suffer with Him, that we may also be glorified together* (Rom. 8:14–17).

BETROTHAL COVENANT

Most Christians know that the church is referred to as the bride of Christ. At the end of the age, He will return to His betrothed and there will be a wedding. The betrothal covenant is one of peace, rest, rule, and reign.

> *And I heard, as it were, the voice of a great multitude, as the sound of many waters and as the sound of mighty thunderings, saying, "Alleluia! For the Lord God Omnipotent reigns! Let us be glad and rejoice and give Him glory, for the marriage of the Lamb has come, and His wife has made herself ready." And to her it was granted to be arrayed in fine linen, clean and bright, for the fine linen is the righteous acts of the saints* (Rev. 19:6–8).

The entire New Testament is full of covenant language. Our Messiah was described as a suffering servant who would walk out the blood covenant of servanthood. He came to restore the friendship of God with His people and showed how to live in friendship with God. He was His Father's Son and He claimed the inheritance that His Father promised Him. He is the Groom that the bride is awaiting. The Renewed/New covenant, through Yeshua, incorporates all these covenants in a new and living way and demonstrates how to walk with God. The Holy Spirit guides us in our walk, and empowers us to testify of the Lord and His truth in this world (Matt. 3:11, John 16:13, Acts 1:8).

COVENANT LIFESTYLES: HOW WE LIVE IN COVENANT

Because most Christians today do not understand the nature of covenants (that they are everlasting), they believe that the only covenant we are to be concerned with is the New covenant/New Testament. If the covenants are everlasting and each covenant includes the preceding covenants, then we are to walk as Yeshua did, fulfilling our part of each of the covenants. We must understand that the Levitical priesthood and its law was established apart from the Sinai covenant in order to remind the people of their sin, foreshadowing the need for the Lamb of God to be slain. Jesus, as Messiah of Israel, became that Lamb of God to restore Israel as the people of God and, through Israel, to restore the whole world. John 3:16 tells us, "For God so loved the world that He gave His only begotten Son, that whoever believes in Him should not perish but have everlasting life." In Matthew 5:17, Yeshua said, "Do not think that I came to destroy the Law [Torah] and the Prophets. I did not come to destroy but to fulfill." It is important that we understand that in the English translation of the New Testament where the "law" is mentioned, it is speaking of either covenant law or Levitical law. Both are contained within the Torah, the first five books of the Bible. What Yeshua was stating in the verse above, concerning the Law/Torah, is that He came to fully explain the Torah and the Prophets by living according to the word of God. To "fulfill" means to fully explain, live, teach and embody the truth of God's word. In Matthew 5:18, He said, "For assuredly, I say to you, till heaven and earth pass away, one jot or one tittle will by no means pass from the law till all is fulfilled." Heaven and earth have not passed away, therefore, neither has the Torah nor the Prophets all been fulfilled.

Yeshua re–established the priesthood after the order of Melchizedek. Hebrews 5:9 emphasizes this, "And having been perfected, He became the author of eternal salvation to all who obey Him, called by God as High Priest 'according to the order of Melchizedek'." In Hebrews 4:14, we are further told that He is our High Priest, "Seeing then that we have a great High Priest who has passed through the heavens, Jesus the Son of God, let us hold fast our confession." Therefore, if He is our High Priest and He is a priest after the order of Melchizedek, then we no longer walk according to the Levitical priesthood. We are a royal priesthood after the order of Melchizedek; The Melchizedek priesthood replaces the Levitical priesthood. We cannot have a High Priest of one order and be of the priesthood of another. 1 Peter 2:9 tells us, "But you are a chosen generation, a royal priesthood, a holy nation, His own special people [. . .]" We are united to Him through faith in the Sacrificial Lamb who was slain for the redemption of mankind.

As members of God's nation (Israel), whether Jews or *grafted in* members, we are in covenant with God. Guided by the Holy spirit, we daily walk (live) by faith in the relationships embraced within each of the covenants. We look with faith and hope to the final marriage relationship with the Lord. Presently, we are engaged or betrothed. Just as on earth, when couples are engaged, they should be nurturing and experiencing the joy of serving each other and forging an intimate and lasting friendship. Our relationship with the Lord follows this same development as we journey by faith through our covenantal walk.

The gospel of salvation is God's plan of redemption for mankind. By redeeming man, God has made it possible to restore His people to a covenant relationship with Him. That relationship allows God to dwell with man in His kingdom when He returns to the earth to set up His kingdom. The gospel of the kingdom must be preached in preparation for this event. In our walk of faith in the Word of God, our relationship with God grows from servanthood to that of marriage.

God has always intended and desired for man to dwell in His presence and under His loving authority. His restoration plan for mankind is for us to return to the relationship with Him as in the original garden, to bring us into His loving presence in the eternal, renewed garden. There we are to dwell forever in His lovingkindness, rest, and peace.

GLOSSARY OF TERMS

Ancient Paths: Jeremiah 6:16 tells us, "Thus says the Lord: 'Stand in the ways and see, and ask for the old paths, where the good way is, and walk in it; then you will find rest for your souls.'" It is believed that our Lord was referring to this passage when He said, "Take My yoke upon you and learn from Me, for I am gentle and lowly in heart, and you will find rest for your souls. For My yoke is easy and My burden light" (Matt. 11:29–30). Jesus was a Rabbi (a teacher) and the way in which a Rabbi would teach the scriptures was called his "yoke". The "ancient paths" spoken of in Jeremiah 6 is a reference to the Torah or the teachings of Moses. Jesus was therefore saying that His yoke, His teaching, was consistent with the "old paths" or "ancient paths", and He was instructing the people to return to those ways.

Day of the Lord: The phrase "day of the LORD" is used throughout the Bible. Joel 2:31 demonstrates this, "The sun shall be turned into darkness, and the moon into blood, before the coming of the great and the terrible day of the LORD." So, does 1 Thessalonians 5:2, "For yourselves know perfectly that the_day of the Lord so comes as a thief in the night." Other examples include Amos 5:18, Obadiah 1:15, Zephaniah 1:7, Acts 2:20, 1 Corinthians 5:5, 2 Corinthians 1:14, 2 Thessalonians 2:1–4, Philippians 1:9–10, Philippians

2:16, and 2 Peter 3:10. The phrase "day of the Lord" usually identifies events that take place at the end of history (Isaiah 7:18–25) and is often closely associated with the phrase "that day." One key in understanding these phrases is to note that they always identify a span of time, during which God personally intervenes in history, directly or indirectly, to accomplish some specific aspect of His plan.

Ephraim: Ephraim was the younger of two sons of Joseph, who was the son of Jacob, whose name God changed to Israel. Ephraim became one of the largest of the twelve tribes of Israel. After King Solomon's death, the twelve tribes split into two distinct kingdoms. Ten of the tribes were called the Northern Kingdom and were also known as Ephraim because it was the largest tribe of the Northern Kingdom. Two tribes formed what is called the Southern Kingdom and is also known as Judah because Judah was the larger of the two tribes. Judah is who we identify as the Jews throughout history thereafter. Ephraim was also known as Israel. The prophets often speak of Israel and Judah meaning the Northern and Southern Kingdoms. The Whole House of Israel would constitute all twelve tribes or both Kingdoms. Ephraim was conquered by Assyria (2 Kings 17) and dispersed and assimilated into the nations (Ezekiel 36:19). They lost their identity as Israel and became identified with the people among whom they had been dispersed. Those who went to France were known as Frenchmen, those to England as Englishmen, and so on. They became known thereafter as the ten lost tribes of Israel. Jesus refers to them in Matthew 15:24, "I was not sent except to the lost sheep of the house of Israel." Because those dispersed had lost their identity as Israelites, when the gospel of salvation was preached to the nations, many of them received it by faith and became Christians. Thereafter,

Christians and the lost ten tribes became one, and included the gentiles who were converted to Christianity.

Fullness of the Gentiles: Romans 11:25 speaks of the fullness of the gentiles, "[. . .] blindness in part has happened to Israel until the fullness of the Gentiles has come in." The fullness of the Gentiles is referring to the faithfulness of the Gentile believers towards Israel (to love Israel). In Romans 11:12 we read, "[. . .] how much more their [Israel's] fullness!" The word fullness is also connected to the completion of Israel's calling, which is to teach Torah to the nations, as opposed to their transgression and failure to do God's will (Rom. 11:12, Rom.11:30). Thus, the fullness of the Gentiles means Gentile believers will be faithful to fulfill their calling toward Israel; returning to the Torah and thereby making Israel jealous (Rom.10:19, Rom. 11:11) thus providing the way for the two houses of Israel, Judah and Israel/Christianity to be reunited and become the whole house of Israel.

Gentile: A Gentile is one who is not in covenant with the God of Israel. Thus, to say one is a Christian gentile is an oxymoron. You cannot be a believer and not a believer at the same time. Paul says that a Gentile who becomes a believer in the God of Israel through Jesus Christ is grafted into Israel and becomes an Israelite. He does not become a Jew, for one must be born a Jew, but through faith in Jesus he is adopted into the family of God, which is Israel. Romans 11:11–24 and Galatians 3:26–29 highlight this. The term "righteous Gentile" has been used by the Jews since the time of the Babylonian captivity to refer to those gentiles/non-Jews who have desired to worship the God of Israel alongside the Jews, within their synagogues. The term continues to be used to identify a non-Jew.

Gospel of Salvation: The proclamation of salvation from the power of sin and death to new, eternal life through faith in the accomplished work of the Lord Jesus Christ (John 3:16–17).

Gospel of the Kingdom: The proclamation of the reign of Jesus Christ as King of Israel over His united people [both Biblical Christianity and Biblical Judaism]; His will on earth as well as His mission to reunite the two kingdoms (Matt. 25:34, Luke 9:2, Luke 4:43, Acts 3:22, Deut. 18:15).

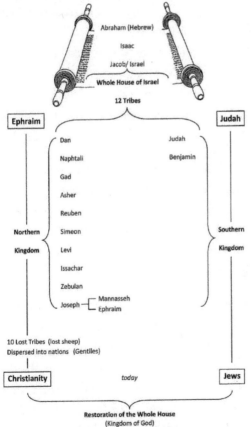

HEBREW/JEW/ISRAELITE/CHRISTIAN

Hebrew: The word Hebrew is first used in the Torah to describe Abraham (Gen. 14:13). It is also taught that the word comes from the word "ābar," which means "the other side," referring to the fact that Abraham came from the other side of the Euphrates. [1]

Jew: The word "Jew" (in Hebrew, "Yehudi") is derived from the name Judah, which was the name of one of Jacob's twelve sons. Judah was the ancestor of one of the tribes of Israel, which was named after him. The term Jew originally referred to members of the tribe of Judah, as distinguished from the other tribes of Israel. Since Abraham was the Great Grandfather of the Jews, the Jews as well as the other tribes of Israel could also be considered Hebrews. The whole house of Israel would be the Hebrew nation.

Israelite: Another name used for the people of God is the children of Israel or Israelites, which refers to the fact that the people are descendants of Jacob, who was also called Israel. Genesis 35:10 says, "And God said to him, 'Your name is Jacob; your name shall not be called Jacob anymore, but Israel shall be your name.'"

Christian: A Christian is one who has, by faith, received Jesus as the Messiah of the God of Israel. Romans 10:9 states, "[. . .] if you confess with your mouth the Lord Jesus and believe in your heart that God has raised Him from the dead, you will be saved." Once a gentile becomes a Christian he/she is grafted into Israel, thereby becoming an Israelite (Romans 11), so that God might have one people, the whole house of Israel.

Jacob's Trouble/Tribulation: The "time of Jacob's trouble" is defined as an unparalleled time in all of history.

Now these are the words that the Lord spoke concerning Israel and Judah. "For thus says the LORD: 'We have heard a voice of trembling, of fear, and not of peace. Ask now, and see, whether a man is ever in labor with child? So why do I see every man with his hands on his loins like a woman in labor, and all faces turned pale? Alas! For that day is great, so that none is like it; and it is the time of Jacob's trouble, but he shall be saved out of it'" (Jer. 30:4–7).

There is no other time like this. Therefore, any other place in scripture claiming this same thing must be talking about the same time (see Daniel 12:1, Matthew 24:15–22, Daniel 9:27, and Revelation 13:5;19:19–20). These are prophetic passages speaking of a future event.

Judaism: There is a distinction made by many, primarily within Christianity, between what is called Biblical Judaism and Rabbinic Judaism. Just as within Christianity there are many different denominations, the same is the case within Judaism. One can get rather complex in defining those distinctions, so in order to keep it as simple as possible we will turn to the words of Jesus.

"Woe to you, scribes and Pharisees, hypocrites! For you are like whitewashed tombs which indeed appear beautiful outwardly, but inside are full of dead men's bones and all uncleanness. Even so you also outwardly appear righteous to men, but inside you are full of hypocrisy and lawlessness" (Matt. 23:27–28).

Lawlessness is the same as Torahlessness. Jesus was speaking to Rabbinic Jews who had added so much man-made tradition to the Torah that they no longer were truly keeping the Torah of God. Biblical Judaism is defined as living the Torah by following the example of the Living Torah who is Jesus Christ. He came to demonstrate how to live and fulfill Torah by walking it out as an example for us. John 1:1 tells us, "In the beginning was the Word, [Torah/Jesus] and the Word [Torah/Jesus] was with God, and the Word [Torah/Jesus] was God." John 1:14 continues, "And the Word [Torah/Jesus] became flesh and dwelt among us [. . .]" John 1:11 concludes, "He came to His own and His own did not receive Him."

Kingdom of God: The kingdom of God is the rule of an eternal sovereign God over all creatures and things. Psalm 103:19 states, "The LORD has established His throne in heaven, and His kingdom rules over all." Daniel 4:3 speaks of the kingdom of God, "How great are His signs, and how mighty His wonders! His kingdom is an everlasting kingdom, and His dominion is from generation to generation." The kingdom of God is also the designation for the sphere of salvation entered into at the new birth. John 3:5–7 records, "Jesus answered, 'Most assuredly, I say to you, unless one is born of water and the Spirit, he cannot enter the kingdom of God." The term is also synonymous with the 'kingdom of heaven.'

Menorah: The menorah is described in the Bible as the seven-lamp (six branches) ancient Hebrew lampstand made of pure gold and used in the portable sanctuary set up by Moses in the wilderness and three hundred years later in the Temple in Jerusalem. Fresh olive oil of the purest quality was burned daily to light its lamps.

Messianic: The term simply means of or relating to the Messiah. Some distinguish between Jews who accept Jesus as their Messiah as Messianic Jews. However, all religious Jews are Messianic in the sense that those who do not believe Jesus to be the promised Messiah are none the less still awaiting the Messiah of Israel. Therefore, it could be reasoned that they are messianic.

MESSIAH/YESHUA/JESUS

Messiah: Messiah from the Hebrew word "Mashiaḥ". in modern Jewish texts in English spelled Mashiach; literally means "anointed one". In Hebrew, the Messiah is often referred to as Melek ha-Mašīaḥ, literally meaning "the Anointed King".[2]

Yeshua: is the Hebrew name given to the Messiah and means "salvation".

Jesus: is the Greek name given to the Messiah.

Millennial: This denotes a period of one thousand years. Within Christianity we often hear about the Millennium or the Millennial Kingdom or the Millennial rule of Christ on the earth. According to descriptions of the kingdom in Isaiah and elsewhere, it will be ruled by Jesus from Jerusalem. It will be characterized by peace as seen in Isaiah 11:9, "They shall not hurt or destroy in all My holy mountain, for the earth shall be full of the knowledge of the LORD as the waters cover the sea."

Mixed Worship: In the days of the kings of Israel, Elijah, the prophet of the God of Israel, was sent to King Ahab to judge the king for making offerings to the false god Baal in the temple of the Lord. Elijah confronted the king, the priests, the prophets, and the people regarding "mixed worship", which is the worship of God along with the worship of false gods; or worshiping God in a manner that He has not prescribed (1 Kings 18). In the days of Jesus, John the Baptist came preaching in the spirit and power of Elijah.

"He will also go before Him in the spirit and power of Elijah, 'to turn the hearts of the fathers to the children,' and the disobedient to the wisdom of the just, to make ready a people prepared for the Lord" (Luke 1:17).

John was very much confronting the Rabbinic Jews for worshiping God according to their traditions rather than according to Torah. Thus, it was the ministry of Elijah once again confronting mixed worship. Elijah is prophesied to come before the return of our Lord and many believe that He will once again prepare the way of the Lord by addressing the mixed worship of our day, both within Christianity and Judaism. Malachi 4:5 says, "Behold, I will send you Elijah the prophet before the coming of the great and dreadful day of the LORD."

Northern Kingdom: After the death of King Solomon, who ruled over the twelve tribes of Israel, the Kingdom was divided into Northern Kingdom and Southern Kingdoms. The Northern Kingdom consisted of ten tribes, also known as Israel and/or the ten lost tribes of Israel, that were scattered into the nations of the world following their defeat by Assyria.

Remnant: The word remnant is used often in the Bible and refers to a group separated out from the whole. We can see this in Isaiah 10:22, "For though your people, O Israel, be as the sand of the sea, a remnant of them will return [. . .]" See Romans 9:27.

Restoration: is the act of restoring; renewal, revival, or reestablishment; the state of being restored; a return of something to a former, original condition.

I will be found by you, says the LORD, and I will bring you back from your captivity; I will gather you from all the nations and from all the places where I have driven you, says the LORD, and I will bring you to the place from which I cause you to be carried away captive (Jer. 29:14).

This is called the Greater Exodus; Isaiah 11:11, "It shall come to pass in that day that the LORD shall set His hand again the second time to recover the remnant of His people who are left [. . .]"

Sabbath: Sabbath is a day set aside for rest and worship. According to Exodus 20:8, the Sabbath is commanded by God to be kept as a holy day of rest, just as God rested from creation. "Remember the Sabbath day, to keep it holy" (Ex. 20:8).

Shofar: A shofar is a musical instrument of ancient origin, made of a horn, traditionally that of a ram, used for Jewish religious purposes.

Southern Kingdom: After the death of King Solomon, who ruled over the twelve tribes of Israel, the kingdom was divided into the Northern Kingdom and Southern Kingdom. The Southern Kingdom consisted of two tribes, Judah and Benjamin. The largest tribe was Judah; therefore, the Southern Kingdom is also known as Judah from which we get the name Jews.

Tanakh: The Hebrew Bible which is also a textual source for the Christian Old Testament. These texts are composed mainly in Biblical Hebrew, with some passages in Biblical Aramaic. The traditional Hebrew text is known as the Masoretic Text, which has three subdivisions. Tanakh is an acronym of the first Hebrew letter of each of the Masoretic Text's three traditional subdivisions: Torah ("Teaching", also known as the Five Books of Moses), Nevi'im ("Prophets"), and Ketuvim ("Writings"), hence TaNaKh.

Torah: "Instruction, Teaching", also called the Pentateuch is the central reference of the religious Judaic tradition. It has a range of meanings. It can most specifically mean the first five books of the Bible, also called the books of Moses. The term Torah means instruction and offers a way of life for those who follow it; it can also mean the continued narrative from Genesis to the end of the Tanakh, and it can even mean the totality of Jewish teaching, culture, and practice. Most commonly it is referring to the first five books of the Bible. It is translated in the New Testament as "law" in the English from the Greek. However, though it contains the law, it is more appropriately called Torah/instruction.

Twelve Tribes: The twelve tribes of Israel constitute "the whole house of Israel" (Ezek. 37:11). Beginning with God desiring to have a nation through which He could bring salvation to the world, He called forth Abraham. Abraham had a son who he named Isaac. Isaac had a son who he named Jacob. God changed Jacob's name to Israel. Israel had twelve sons and from those twelve sons come the twelve tribes of Israel.

Yahweh: is a form of the Hebrew name for their God used in the Bible. The name came to be regarded by Jews (300 BC) as too sacred to be spoken, and the vowel sounds are uncertain. Yahveh is another spelling for the name.

Zion: Psalm 87:2–3 says, "The Lord loves the gates of Zion more than all the other dwellings of Jacob. Glorious things are spoken of you, O city of God!" According to this verse, Zion is synonymous with city of God, and it is a place that God loves. Zion is Jerusalem. Mount Zion is the high hill on which David built a citadel. It is on the southeast side of the city. The word Zion is also used in a theological or spiritual sense in Scripture. In the Old Testament, Zion refers figuratively to Israel as the people of God (Isaiah 60:14). In the New Testament, Zion refers to God's spiritual kingdom.

BIBLIOGRAPHY

CHAPTER 11:

[1] Challies, Tim, *The Discipline of Spiritual Discernment*, Illinois: Crossway, 2008.

CHAPTER 13:

[1] Vine, W.E., Unger, Merrill F., and White Jr., William, *Vine's Expository Dictionary of Old and New Testament Words*, Thomas Nelson, 1996.

[2] *Webster's New World College Dictionary*. 5th Edition, 2016.

[3] *Collins English Dictionary-Complete and Unabridged*, 12th Edition, Harper Collins, 2014.

CHAPTER 14:

[1] Strong, James, *Strong's Exhaustive Concordance of the Bible*, Massachusetts: Hendrickson Publishers, 2007.

[2] Strong, James, *Strong's Exhaustive Concordance of the Bible*, Massachusetts: Hendrickson Publishers, 2007.

[3] Talmud, b.B.Bat.21a.

[4] Talmud, b.B.Bat.21a.

CHAPTER 15:

[1] Prophecy Headlines. Accessed April 12, 2017. http:// prophecynewsstand.blogspot.com.

CHAPTER 16:

[1] Elwell, Walter A., Ed. *Evangelical Dictionary of Theology*. 2nd Edition, Michigan: Baker Academic, 2001.

[2] Strong, James, *Strong's Exhaustive Concordance of the Bible*, Massachusetts: Hendrickson Publishers, 2007.

[3] Strong, James, *Strong's Exhaustive Concordance of the Bible*, Massachusetts: Hendrickson Publishers, 2007.

[4] 119 Ministries. "Misunderstood Verses of the New Testament." http://www.119ministries.com.

[5] Andrews, J.N., *History of the Sabbath*. Accessed April 12, 2017. http://www.sabbathtruth.com/portals/20/documents/History_of_the_Sabbath.pdf.

[6] Bacchiocchi, Samuele, "The Rise of Sunday Observance in Early Christianity," in *The Sabbath in Scripture and History*, ed. Kenneth A. Strand (Washington, D.C.: Review and Herald 1982).

[7] Living Word Ministries. "Living Word Ministries." http://www.lwm.net.

[8] Garr, John, "Hebraic Heritage Christian Center." www.restorationfoundation.org.

[9] Heidler, Robert D. *The Messianic Church Arising!*, Glory of Zion International Ministries, 2006.

CHAPTER 17:

[1] Strong, James, *Strong's Exhaustive Concordance of the Bible*, Massachusetts: Hendrickson Publishers, 2007.

[2] Strong, James, *Strong's Exhaustive Concordance of the Bible*, Massachusetts: Hendrickson Publishers, 2007.

[3] Archer Jr., Gleason L., Harris, R. Laird, Waltke, Bruce K., *Theological Woodbook of the Old Testament*, Moody Publishers, 1980.

CHAPTER 18:

[1] Fausset, Andrew Robert. *Fausset's Bible Dictionary,* http://www.bible-history.com/faussets/. Public Domain.

GLOSSARY OF TERMS:

[1] Archer Jr., Gleason L., Harris, R. Laird, Waltke, Bruce K., *Theological Woodbook of the Old Testament,* Moody Publishers, 1980.

[2] Archer Jr., Gleason L., Harris, R. Laird, Waltke, Bruce K., *Theological Woodbook of the Old Testament,* Moody Publishers, 1980.

CPSIA information can be obtained
at www.ICGtesting.com
Printed in the USA
LVHW042008070219
606816LV00001B/10/P